KATIE

UP AND DOWN
THE HALL

KATIE

UP AND DOWN THE HALL

*The True Story of
How One Dog Turned Five
Neighbors into a Family*

GLENN PLASKIN

CENTER
STREET

New York Boston Nashville

Center Street
Hachette Book Group
237 Park Avenue
New York, NY 10017

www.centerstreet.com

Center Street is a division of Hachette Book Group, Inc.
The Center Street name and logo are trademarks of Hachette Book Group, Inc.

The Hachette Speakers Bureau provides a wide range of authors for speaking events. To find out more, go to www.hachettespeakersbureau.com or call (866) 376-6591.

The publisher is not responsible for websites (or their content) that are not owned by the publisher.

Printed in the United States of America

Originally published in hardcover by Hachette Book Group.

First Trade Edition: May 2012
10 9 8 7 6 5 4 3 2 1

The Library of Congress has cataloged the hardcover edition as follows:
Plaskin, Glenn.
    Katie up and down the hall: the true story of how one dog turned five neighbors into a family / Glenn Plaskin. — 1st ed.
        p. cm.
    Summary: "The heartwarming true story of how one special cocker spaniel turned five strangers into family" — Provided by publisher.
    ISBN 978-1-59995-254-3
  1. Cocker spaniels — New York (State) — New York — Biography.
2. Plaskin, Glenn.   3. Human-animal relationships — New York (State) — New York.   4. Neighbors — New York (State) — New York — Biography.   5. Strangers — New York (State) — New York — Biography.
6. Families — New York (State) — New York.   7. Battery Park City (New York, N.Y.) — Biography.   8. New York (N.Y.) — Biography.
9. Battery Park City (New York, N.Y.) — Social life and customs.
10. New York (N.Y.) — Social life and customs.   I. Title.
    SF429.C55P55 2010
    636.70092'9 — dc22
                                                        2009053413

ISBN 978-1-59995-256-7 (pbk.)

To Mom, Dad, and to my sister Debby—
with much love and gratitude for always being there.

CONTENTS

ACKNOWLEDGMENTS

People often say that writing is a lonely, isolating profession.

And it can be, though I've never really experienced it that way.

I guess it's because I'm always bouncing ideas (and multiple drafts) off of my patient circle of friends, family, and colleagues, and of course, my editor.

In this, the most personal book I've ever written, I was lucky to have so many wise souls on my side—and on the other end of the phone.

First, heartfelt thanks to Harry Helm, my dog-loving editor at the Hachette Book Group, whose insight, love of the subject, and incisive editing have been altogether indispensable. Without Harry encouraging me to write this at our fateful first lunch, there would be no book. Harry and his able team in both New York and Nashville—including Shanon Stowe, Pamela Clements, Jody Waldrup, Adlai Yeomans, Gina Wynn, Chris Murphy, Martha Otis, Kelly Leonard, Valerie Russo, Kallie Shimek, Jaime Slover, and Karen Torres—have done a fantastic job making this book come alive.

As always, I'm grateful to my supersonic agents, the great Jan Miller, a dear friend and fellow animal lover who encouraged me to strike out in a new direction, and the vivacious and efficient Nena Madonia, wise beyond her years. Together with the entire gang at Dupree Miller, they did a superlative job.

I am greatly indebted to my longtime friend and editorial advisor, Ed Friedel, who provided invaluable suggestions, insight, and advice on each succeeding draft of the manuscript as well as meticulous corrections. His is a rare talent.

In addition, I'm very lucky to have worked with publicists Lynn Goldberg and Angela Hayes, both unforgettable in their strategic devotion and vision for *Katie*.

I must also turn back in time and pay tribute to my longtime magazine editor, Ellen Stoianoff, who loved Katie and supported the original idea for the "Granny Down the Hall" article. She would have been so delighted to see the entire story told.

A strong memory is never quite enough when writing a true-life story, so I'm also beholden to the many people who witnessed the events I describe and further illuminated them for me by sharing precious anecdotes, recollections, and details.

First and foremost, I was fortunate to draw from the memories of John Freed, and his son, Ryan, two starring figures here, who shared their firsthand reminiscences, providing an intimate link to the seven-year period they lived down the hall from me.

Next, I am thankful to Michael Simon, who generously reviewed the manuscript, providing keen observations on the people he'd known so well, and to Paul Huberdeau, who contributed crucial details to later chapters in the book.

Equally essential were the contributions of Michael Gordon, a once-in-a-lifetime friend and sage adviser. His impeccable memory was especially helpful in writing chapter fourteen.

In addition, I was greatly aided by the kindness of Naia Kheladze, Lee Blake, Rose Dicker, and Helene Meltzer, each of whom provided extended interviews about events outside my own firsthand experience.

Many thanks also for the perspectives provided by Scott Simon DMV (Katie's vet), Stuart Cohen, Jeffrey Cohen, Ramon Aizarna, Barry Meltzer, Bea Aron, Norah Berner, Anita Diggle, Robert Simko, Manny Norona, Robert Defendorf, and our building's doormen, Felipe Dominguez and Dave Scott-Duns.

I'm also grateful to my close friend Brandon Williams and to Diego Costa for producing the Katie book trailer—a project that would not have happened were it not for book marketing expert John Kremer. I am so thankful to my friend Ann McIndoo for introducing John to me.

And thanks also to web designers Chris Matthias and Dan Root for creating katiebook.com.

And a special nod to Eileen Calvanese, horticulturist for the Battery Park City Parks Conservancy, who enlightened me about the plantings and landscaping of our neighborhood.

Finally, I am touched and grateful for the close friends and colleagues who have lavished their support on me. They include a brilliant team of "coaches," Peg Wallis, Dr. Paul Weinfeld, Eric Mugele, and Mike Mole; the incomparable Owen Laster; the intrepid Susan Grode; my "youngest" friend, Bud Klauber; the always faithful Gregory Dickow; Michael Darvin; Freda Hertz; Scott Parris; Jason VanOra; Marvin Feuerstein; Jack Plaskin; Linda Belfer; Rob Rabin, David Winner, Dan Strone, Robby Baker, Paul Donzella, Bunny Shestack, Ellen Kruse, Geraldine McBride, Norah Berner, Norman Goldstein, Harvey Helfand, Jeff Schoenheit, Susan Ungaro, Vincent Smetana,

Mickey Alam Khan, Harvey Moskowitz, Stuart Avrick, Sy and Esther Kornblau, and Justin Weinberg, to name only a few.

And, finally, a special thank you to Anthony Robbins, a true friend of the heart who has generously contributed to my understanding of the universal need for love and connection. Tony, better than anyone, taught me about the driving force of emotion and the "power of proximity," two principles that have everything to do with the events that unfold in this book.

KATIE
UP AND DOWN
THE HALL

Welcome to Battery Park City

Tucked away at the southernmost tip of Manhattan is a little town built on water.

Many New Yorkers are only vaguely aware of it, while tourists often pass it by. In fact, the charm of the place is that it's so hidden away, though impossible to leave once you've discovered it.

Armies of gardeners maintain the winding trails, manicured parks, and gardens splashed with flowers of every color.

Here there are playgrounds decorated with fanciful sculptures, playing fields brimming with Little Leaguers, expansive lawns for sunbathing, duck ponds with waterfalls, and restaurants perched along the water.

Then there are the plazas for outdoor concerts, the marina filled with motorboats and yachts, and the spectacular Winter Garden, a glass-enclosed pavilion featuring sixteen palm trees overlooking the Hudson.

And best of all, day or night, it's the water lapping up against the shore that you hear, not sirens or cars, a fact appreciated by us writers.

The idea for it all began in the late 1960s with the

construction of the World Trade Center. The excavation for those soaring 110-story Twin Towers produced a gargantuan amount of earth. And like chefs not wasting any of their leftover ingredients, construction crews saved tons of the dirt, rocks, and sand for a greater purpose.

It took six years to complete, but ingenious engineers devised a way to use this material as landfill, filling in the Hudson to create a brand-new town. Water was pumped out, new earth was put in, and the boundary line of the river was pushed westward—creating a ninety-two-acre oasis thereafter known as Battery Park City.

The result is a sleek virtual city—with sparkling sand-colored high-rises flanked by office towers, hotels, museums, movie theaters, public schools, and a shopping arcade, all of it set on thirty-six leafy acres of open space.

And it's in this place—a fledgling waterfront town—that our story begins.

I moved here twenty-five years ago, seduced by the spectacular views of New York Harbor, historic Ellis Island, and New Jersey's "gold coast," though people questioned my migrating to a "wilderness" that was little more than a sandy beachhead.

Getting to the local subway station required what amounted to aerobic exercise. One uptown friend joked he'd need a passport, a bike, or a jogging suit to visit. True, we were inconvenient to get to and had exactly one supermarket, one drug store, one dry cleaner, one bank, and a half-finished garden and pool.

But to me the Hudson River sunsets, up-close views of the Statue of Liberty, and the never-ending parade of boats made it all worth it. After all, I'd come from a dark walk-up apartment overlooking an airshaft!

Compared to that, my new Battery Park City home seemed

utterly sublime. It was filled with sunlight and perched so low to the water that I felt as if I was living on a riverboat. I had my own honey locust tree that pushed up against the living room window, enveloping the entire space and creating a tree house effect.

And being a pioneer in Battery Park City had other advantages too. Since my neighbors and I were isolated on the same little block of land, we were constantly bumping into each other, unavoidably so.

In a notoriously brusque city of eight million, where neighbors typically keep their distance, our community of 9,000 was an unusually open one—with people mingling at neighborhood block parties, outdoor picnics, pick-up basketball games, and sailboat outings—happy to be living in what amounts to an idyllic resort town.

The backbone of it all is a magnificent tree-lined Esplanade, a 1.2-mile promenade winding its way around the entire length of the Battery. All the buildings and outdoor spaces here are set along this expansive walkway like pearls on a string.

In the warm days of early fall, the grand English oaks, river birches, and weeping willows sway in the wind. As I bike through the pathways, I'm shaded by a lush umbrella of trees, an ideal backdrop for lunchtime strollers. In the evening, the purple lanterns set close to the water glow as residents and visitors dine at candlelit tables.

In winter, though, living here becomes a grueling marathon, a regimen of ice, wind, and snow. Blustery high winds seep through our windows. Snow floating down on the Statue of Liberty turns it into a snow globe. And I'm always mesmerized by the jagged ice chunks traveling downriver, their edges catching the sun as the current moves them briskly along.

Then, with the arrival of spring, the neighborhood perks

up once again. Cherry blossoms and silver lindens perfume the air with their heady sweetness. Eighty species of birds flutter amid the lion's tails, roses, azaleas, anemones, toad lilies, and lavender hydrangeas. And hopeful fishermen cast their lines into the Hudson for local specialties like bluefish, white perch, winter flounder, and tomcod.

But best of all, the Hudson River is overflowing with sailboats, private yachts, tour boats, Jet Skis, and kayaks—plus barges, water taxis, and commuter ferries—a blur of nautical movement creating a wild dance across the water.

Most dramatic are the mammoth cruise ships that glide southward to the ocean as people stand on shore and wave. The only thing I haven't seen on the Hudson is somebody floating by in a bathtub.

On land, the Esplanade is jam-packed with bikers, joggers, rollerbladers, skateboarders, picnickers, volleyball and soccer players, and a cavalcade of baby carriages. This is Kid Central, with toddlers and elementary school kids everywhere—their bikes, skateboards, frisbees, and kites filling the neighborhood with action.

And that's not to mention the *dogs*—hundreds of them in every shape and size. Majestic Great Danes rub noses with pint-sized pugs and Shih Tzus. Golden retrievers and Labs race by the river, pulling their owners, trailing behind bikes, or staying ahead of Baby Jogger strollers. German shepherds, Labradoodles, Westies, beagles, and puggles parade along the water, sniffing under trees and reveling in the sun. At the nearby dog run, boxers, Yorkies, poodles, Boston terriers, Wheatens, and bulldogs chase balls and one other, or splash in the dunking pool.

It's a circus and a dog show rolled up in one. And it's perfect employment for the neighborhood's dog walkers, exercising their troops from dawn to dusk.

But to say that the neighborhood is dog friendly would be an understatement. At Halloween, canine residents compete in the neighborhood's annual costume contest and dog parade. Contestants have included a Batman whippet, a *Wizard of Oz* cowardly lion Bernese mountain dog, a Cinderella Chihuahua, a Minnie Mouse pug, and a Madonna Lhasa apso, all strutting their stuff.

They competed against creatively attired Rhodesian ridgebacks, Australian shepherds, dalmatians, Havaneses, Border collies, Scottish terriers, and, of course, an army of mutts. (One year, the champion was Santiago, a one-year-old pit bull "biker"—in a leather jacket, leather cap, white T-shirt, and blue jeans.)

∽

It was in this dog-friendly world that my own cocker spaniel, Katie, found a home. Over a period of nearly fifteen years (via more than 20,000 walks) my curiously intelligent dog explored every inch of Battery Park City.

I can see her now—trotting along the Hudson, racing for tennis balls in the park, chasing squirrels, snoozing under a willow tree, stealing nacho chips at our local Mexican restaurant, taking sunset cruises on a local sailboat, greedily licking my pistachio ice-cream cone on a hot summer night, and, like all dogs, searching for the best smells and tastiest treats available to her.

But this is not just a story about a precocious dog.

It's about how that dog had the power to turn five neighbors into a real family—racing up and down a 120-foot hallway between apartments, pushing doors in with her paws, herding her "pack" together, and trotting outside along the Hudson, her spirit a magnet to all.

Through her soulful eyes, we witness antics and family adventures spanning everything from Hollywood high times to the terrors of 9/11, one dog creating a family circle that embraced and transformed each of its members, including me.

Of course, none of what I'm about to tell you was planned—or expected. In fact, I sometimes ask myself: What if I had never moved to Battery Park City at all? Was everything that happened just an accident, coincidence, or luck?

Or was it fate and destiny?

I can tell you I definitely believe in the power of *proximity*, for who we're physically near is so often who we wind up being close to.

And so, I now invite you to enter my little world in a town built on water.

Like one of those online maps that allows you to zoom into any city, then zero in on the neighborhood, street, and building, come on down to Battery Park City...and find out what happened—*up and down the hall*.

New York
May 2010

CHAPTER ONE

Faux-Paws

As a kid, I was never a "dog person," to say the least. In fact, I was terrified of dogs.

It all began with "Strippy"—a menacing black-and-white spotted English pointer, who was always barking furiously at the top of his lungs in our neighbor's yard.

There he was, all seventy pounds of him, nervously pacing back and forth on a long metal chain, or sitting ominously on top of his green-and-white doghouse, surveying his kingdom from above.

Strippy was the king of the mountain—and I was his prey, frightened by his incessant barking and growling. We might as well have been living next door to a *lion*, for to me it amounted to the same thing.

On hot summer days on Bondcroft Drive, a quiet street in a suburb of Buffalo, New York, my sister Joanne and I would race through the sprinkler or splash in a small wading pool. But we weren't entirely carefree, always keeping a wary eye on this seemingly dangerous animal, just thirty feet away.

I would later understand that the source of Strippy's frustration was being chained up all day. After all, pointers are full of energy and go-power, tireless as hard-driving hunting dogs. They love to gallop and roam.

So it was no wonder that Strippy was so high-strung, lacking freedom and exercise. His owners kept him restrained, they said, to prevent him from running away.

One day, when I was about four years old, I was playing in the hedges behind our house with my sister, then six. In a flash, out of nowhere, Strippy suddenly broke loose and tore out of his yard and into ours, racing over the hedges and straight toward us.

Strippy pushed us down to the ground with his huge paws, bouncing on top of us, though not actually scratching or hurting us in any way. In hindsight, he was probably just being friendly and knocked us down by accident. But tell that to two petrified kids.

My heart was pounding furiously as I felt the horrible weight of that dog on top of me before he raced away from the yard.

My mom saw it all from the bedroom window, and by the time she came rushing outside, we were cowering in the bushes, crying and hysterical. I escaped into a large cardboard box that was nearby on the lawn, shivering inside it, while my sister huddled in Mom's arms.

This traumatic event would stay with us for years. Thereafter, any time a friendly neighborhood dog trotted by, we froze in our tracks, like statues, paralyzed by fear.

But by the time I was ten, this fear of dogs had miraculously faded away, thanks to "Lady," a vivacious beagle who became our neighborhood mascot. I never can forget her adorable face, those floppy brown ears, and expressive brown eyes that literally sparkled. True, she was a little chubby, but that didn't stop her from being the spunkiest dog I'd ever seen.

She'd race us around the yard—her long tail waving back and forth like a windshield wiper—chasing balls, leaping into the air, tagging behind me on bike rides, fetching branches, begging for snacks, and snooping into everything—overjoyed to play with the neighborhood kids and stealing kisses with her long tongue. I loved it when she'd roll over, desperate to have her stomach rubbed.

It wasn't long before I wanted a dog of my own. But Mom was firmly opposed to it. By now, I had another sister, Debby, and Mom said that raising three kids was enough work—that we weren't meant to have a dog.

Yet, as a girl, Mom had treasured a white poodle named Sadie, and later, a German shepherd named Duke. Her father, our Papa, was a great dog lover and lobbied on my behalf. The arguments went on for weeks. But the answer was still no.

Not to be dissuaded, my stubborn grandfather forged ahead, and one morning simply showed up at our house with a miniature schnauzer.

Mom was furious. By the time I got home from school, the black puppy, named Herman, was tied to the swing set in the backyard, looking up at me with a plaintive expression that said: "*Keep me.*"

But inside, Mom and Papa were having a heated "discussion."

Much as I begged, Mom wouldn't allow him to stay. Papa took the dog away—and that was it for me and dogs for decades.

⌒⌒

Well into adulthood, though, I always kept a *to-do* list tucked into my date book. It had life goals (and trivia) written out on it: work objectives, hobby ideas, good restaurants, a list of friends and phone numbers, and for twenty-five years running, a three-word *note to self*: GET A DOG.

I somehow sensed that having a four-legged companion would turn out to be one of the secrets to contentment (and sometimes easier to find than a two-legged one).

Meanwhile, also on my to-do list was the goal of upgrading my living situation. After six years, I couldn't stand the claustrophobic, dark apartment on the Upper East Side—a cross between a cave and a prison. I was desperate for something better.

In the spring of 1985, after weeks of looking at outrageously priced high-rise apartments, just as an afterthought, my realtor suggested that I check out a brand-new building in Battery Park City. It had unobstructed Hudson River views, a swimming pool, gardens, restaurants, and stores. If it was too good to be true—*and* a real bargain—that was because not many people back then wanted to live at the southern tip of Manhattan, so far from midtown.

But after I saw the Hudson River rolling by what would be my new living room window, I didn't care *how* far out of the way it was.

Once I was settled into Battery Park City, though, my sunny new apartment seemed awfully quiet—and once again, the impulse to get a dog came and went.

That impulse to get a dog was amped up by the sheer power of suggestion. In our complex of 1,720 apartments (spread out in six cement-and-glass buildings, including a trio of thirty-five-story high rises), we had more than 300 dogs.

The Esplanade and dog run were more jam-packed than the LA freeways.

So why was I still tooling along alone?

Admittedly, I'd always been consumed with work and work alone, focused on a career that had often become a blinding obsession.

Two years earlier, I'd had my first book published, a

comprehensive biography of Vladimir Horowitz that took three years to write; and after that, between freelancing at a women's magazine and working a full-time job at a men's lifestyle publication, I'd found my leisure time limited. And the little of it that I had was somewhat empty.

No matter how much surface excitement I felt meeting celebrity interview subjects—or covering stories like the America's Cup in Bermuda, a rodeo in Denver, or a Christmas chat at the White House with Nancy Reagan—there was, just underneath, a pervasive sense of loneliness. And nothing could chase it away.

Admittedly, I wasn't great at establishing intimate relationships—though I did have a wide circle of close friends. Yet it seemed to me that creating a stronger domestic life was key to creating a happier life. Could the prime part of that new life be a canine companion?

Over the next two years, every time I was tempted to get a dog, I pulled back, distracted by yet more work or anxious at confronting a new learning curve. After all, what did I know about owning a dog? What breed to buy? How to train it?

All of it seemed overwhelming—until 1987, when I finally took the plunge.

One hot summer day, I was out shopping for clothes with a longtime friend, Michael, an architect and designer who had moved into our apartment building on my suggestion. He had an unerring eye and had helped me get my Battery Park City apartment in order.

That humid day, as we browsed around in Bloomingdale's, I was looking for bathing suits—not puppies.

But afterward, as we were taking a walk up Lexington Avenue, we came upon a pet store on East 77th Street. The front windows were filled with frolicking pups.

"Oh, look!" Michael exclaimed, spotting just the one he liked. "There's an incredibly cute pug."

In the front was a tiny tan dog with a wrinkly face and a pushed-in nose, contentedly biting a toy mouse.

I was only half-listening to Michael as he went on: "I love all the Chinese dogs," he said (perhaps viewing them as much as décor-enhancers as pets). "There are the Pekingeses, the Japanese chins, Shih Tzus, Chinese cresteds…." And having accessorized rooms with dogs in sculptural form, he joked, "And they make wonderful porcelains too."

Yikes. I was beginning to get worried by that excited smile on Michael's face. I'd seen it before, when he'd suggested buying a dining table that was well beyond my means.

So, staring at the little pug, I muttered, "He's cute." Michael practically yanked me into the store, and the rest of what happened is a blur.

Within fifteen minutes of being down on the floor playing inside a metal pen with the pug, Michael, no stranger to high-end retail, announced to the clerk, "Wrap him up…we'll take him," as if we were buying a couch. *We*, of course, meant *me*.

I pulled out my credit card to cover the price, which didn't include his crate, toys, pillows, food and water bowls, blankets, deodorizers, shampoo, conditioner, and baby gate.

The taxi ride home was surreal, me holding my shopping bags, Michael holding "Baby," the name he'd instantly given the pug.

Back at my apartment, we set up the puppy's new headquarters in my kitchen, and I can still see Michael dancing with him, holding Baby up by his front paws while the back paws strutted away. Well, at least they were happy.

A few hours later Michael said good night and went back

upstairs to the twenty-third floor. There I was, left alone on the third floor with my purchase.

Baby was in his crate, snoring away in the kitchen, and I was lying in my crate in a panic, nearly hyperventilating—sweating and anxious. I felt trapped by the consequences of my rash decision. It reminded me of the time I got arrested for speeding. I started calling up friends, "I've made a real mistake...what was I thinking?"

I knew, instinctively, that Baby was the wrong dog for me. I didn't want a breed this small, didn't want a male, and didn't want a dog that snored either. Other than that, Baby was perfect.

"You're in shock," said Michael. "Just give yourself a chance. Don't make any quick decisions." But I already had.

I called him at the crack of dawn the next day and said, "I can't do it. The dog is going back..."

And off I went, back to the pet store. I felt really guilty about it as Baby had a rather worried expression on his face, maybe sensing that he was heading back to the store window. But because he was such a beautiful dog, I reasoned that someone would come along and buy him.

And so it was that Baby was in my life for less than twenty-four hours.

Bye-bye baby.

$$\sim$$

After that false start, a year passed, though I hadn't given up on the idea of getting a dog. I was just stalled.

What I really needed and luckily found was a *mentor*, someone who could calmly and wisely lead me in the right dog direction.

Fortuitously, in the spring of 1988, I became friendly with Joe, an extroverted long-time resident of my building who worked as a bartender across the street at the Marriott Hotel.

Loquacious and curious, Joe could talk to *anybody*—while he also had a great talent turning a house into a home with a beautiful apartment on the twenty-third floor. He was a meticulous caretaker as well, completely devoted to his three-year-old cocker spaniel named Dinah.

Like most classically groomed cocker spaniels, Dinah had a "full skirt," long blond hair that flowed from her torso to the ground, which reminded me of a carpet sweeper. She had a plaintive oval face (a canine Modigliani), melancholy brown eyes, and a submissive disposition—nothing like the lusty personality of Lady, but sweet and demure.

Joe was admittedly a tough taskmaster. He had trained Dinah to obey his every command—no pulling on the leash, no stealing treats from the table, no snooping on the ground (keeping her long ears clean), and no accidents on the carpet. She even had to face uphill when relieving herself, so that her fur would not get wet!

Joe would erupt with a harsh rebuke and a swat on Dinah's butt if she committed any such infractions.

Because he was such a disciplinarian, Dinah, I noticed, seemed a little afraid of him, not wanting to disappoint. She'd look up at him with a worried nervous expression and I felt sorry for her. Like some dog owners (not the kind I turned out to be!), Joe was the commander, deeply caring but strict—and Dinah was his servant.

Joe could be affectionate too—kissing Dinah, rewarding her with treats, patting her on the head for excellent behavior, and grooming her to the nth degree.

I'd often find him showcasing his talents outside on the Esplanade, brushing out Dinah's ears and expertly trimming her coat with an electric clipper as she sat perfectly still on a park bench.

One day, something stirred inside me as I watched Joe perfecting Dinah's pendulous ears. I was so taken by those ears, which, in the end, turned out to be the key to moving forward.

Joe noticed. "You ought to get a cocker spaniel," he told me, stroking Dinah's back with a wiry brush and then putting the final touches on her coat with a portable hair dryer. "You've got to get one. It would be good for you."

CHAPTER TWO

Test-Run Dog

My mentor was turning out to be a true friend and a well-intentioned know-it-all.

Joe loved taking me under his wing and giving advice on anything and everything—from dating and dining to shopping tips, family relationships, and social networking. And I was more than receptive to Joe's guidance and friendship—as I had more time on my hands than I was used to.

A few years earlier, I had quit my full-time magazine job when the freelance work picked up, which included the strong prospect of collaborating with a pop star on his autobiography. But the book idea hadn't panned out. And when my regular magazine gig dried up as well, I was actively looking for another full-time job while battling a sense of loneliness at home.

"You need some company—and getting a dog is a lot quicker than a dating service," he joked, talking nonstop like a used car salesman for the next week about the virtues of cockers.

"They're so calm, friendly, easy to train—and pretty too. How many people do you know who are like *that*?!"

"And," he exclaimed, without taking a breath, "a dog is a

real magnet—you walk around with a cute one—and you'll get one just like it."

But the main benefit of being a pet owner, he said, was the incomparable companionship from it, something he especially needed. While, by night, Joe tended bar, he was alone much of the day, just like me, so he understood the feeling of being isolated. His basic cure-all was the magic of owning a dog.

"Maybe you're right," I said carefully, always the cautious one. "I'll tell you what. Why don't you *loan* Dinah out to me for an afternoon—so I can take her out for a test drive?"

"Like rent-a-dog?!" he laughed, game to try my scheme.

"Exactly. Dinah will be my test-run dog."

So I took her home with me, first for a long walk outside and then inside for a joint nap. Honestly, I had never had a dog in my bed (at least not a canine one) and having her lean against me as we snoozed was an incredible sensation. It was so relaxing. I later read that a dog's presence can actually lower your heart rate and blood pressure. It certainly was doing something for me.

I napped in a way I rarely had, resting more deeply than usual, my breath following hers. Anyone who has ever slept with a dog knows exactly what I'm talking about. It was comforting and cozy. And I was touched by Dinah's gentleness and by the way she drew next to me, putting her paws on my arm.

After a few more test naps, I was sold. And over the next few weeks, Joe began giving me a crash course on how to prepare for a puppy of my own.

"Now you're going to need a kennel…." he lectured, his intense blue eyes pinning me with detailed instructions. "Your puppy is going to view this enclosed space as its own little home. You put some soft towels on the bottom of it with a pillow and you're set. The beauty of it is that a puppy will never soil its pen if it can possibly avoid it. You'll put the crate in the kitchen, put up a baby fence, then leave the door of the crate open with the floor of the kitchen covered in newspaper or wee-wee pads."

"Wee-wee *what*?" I asked. "This sounds like more work than having a real baby."

"Oh, it's going to be," Joe promised. "Just wait. Having a puppy is a full-time job. Every two hours your dog needs to be picked up and taken outside so it gets the idea that relieving itself in the house is not an option. The puppy needs to be close to you, to be able to smell you, because it's going to be missing its litter mates and mom. *You're* his new mom!"

One day, as he continued pressuring me about getting a dog, I blurted out, "You're driving me nuts!" With his typical acerbic wit, he answered, "Mmmmm...not a very far drive."

Furthermore, Joe told me that, while he would be happy to support my efforts in training a dog, there was an older woman living just a few doors down from me on the third floor who was an experienced cocker spaniel owner as well. "She's the perfect person to talk to, and you should definitely meet," he said.

"Her name is Pearl and her dog, Brandy, recently died. This would help both of you. When I'm not around, you can go to her and she'll give you great advice."

Although I had lived in the building for three years, I had never exchanged anything except for a casual "hello" with any of the seventeen tenants living along our 120-foot hallway. All that was about to change.

A few days later, Joe came over to my apartment and took me down the hall for an introduction to his friend. This would turn out to be the most important thing that Joe would ever do for me—and the kindest. I could never have guessed that this casual little introduction would so completely change my life.

The door opened and there was Pearl, a solid-looking seventy-six-year-old with military posture, a sparkle in her eye, and a majestic high forehead with a mane of lustrous gray hair. There was something warm and homey about her, yet at the same time, I noticed a no-nonsense quality that spelled impressive strength. Not the perfume and jewelry type, Pearl was dressed in black pants and a gray cable-knit sweater, a cake pan in her hands, her sweater smudged with flour.

Dinah led the way into the apartment, her tail wagging.

"Hello baby girl! How's my little Dinah?" cooed Pearl, pulling a box of biscuits she kept on hand for such occasions from a nearby bookcase. She bent down to give one to Dinah, but the dog hesitated, tentatively looking up at Joe for the go-ahead. With a nod of his head, Dinah gently pulled it from Pearl's hand and trotted happily away with it.

Pearl's own cocker, Brandy, had died the year before at age twelve, and she greatly missed her, though I would discover that Pearl was not one to reveal her emotions easily. Stoic and private, she pushed aside her loss and now enjoyed Dinah's company whenever she came to visit.

"So, Joe, you smelled my plum tart and decided to come my way," she laughed, ushering us in.

"Definitely. Pearl, I want to introduce you to my friend— and your neighbor—Glenn. I thought you two should get to know each other."

"I'm no longer dating!" winked Pearl, firmly shaking my hand. She was so down-to-earth and easy to talk to, and I liked her from the minute I saw that plum tart, which turned out to be scrumptious. She cut into it, put some whipped cream on top, and we were good to go.

Next, Pearl introduced me to her husband, Arthur, a retired women's apparel salesman, about eighty at the time, contentedly lounging on a gray velour armchair, his feet propped up on the matching ottoman, reading the newspaper. He was dressed in what turned out to be his daily uniform—a red plaid bathrobe, blue pajamas, and leather slippers.

"How do you do?" he grinned, leaning up toward me to offer a very firm handshake. "Glad to finally meet one of the neighbors."

"Dinah," Arthur boomed, "over here!" he said, taking off his reading glasses to get a better look and then pulling her onto his lap. "That's a good girl," he said, stroking her ears.

Pearl explained that they had moved to Battery Park City two years earlier from a country house in Red Hook, in upstate Dutchess County, New York, because they wanted a more compact home—"no more mowing that grass," laughed Arthur—and loved being so close to the water.

"He never mowed it much anyway," whispered Pearl, in an aside to Joe.

I noticed, even this first time we met, that there was an easy affection between the couple, Arthur touching Pearl's arm, gently brushing her shoulder. I liked the way they teased one another—a rib here, a jab there, all in good humor. This was a pleasure to see after no less than *fifty* years of marriage.

"And we're still talking," laughed Pearl.

"And she's still cooking," Arthur answered.

Like Pearl herself, the apartment's furnishings were practical and down-to-earth, anything but fancy, with heavy mahogany furniture, a worn brown-and-rust-flowered sectional sofa, and a small dining room table set in the middle of the combination living room–dining room, typical of many Manhattan apartments.

Everything was a bit dusty and worn, but it was cozy, with

botanical prints, flowers, potted palms, and a forest of plants lining the windowsill, livening things up.

As we sat there getting acquainted, I was struck by Pearl's wit and quick humor.

"So, Joe is talking you into real trouble," she smirked.

"Yes, I am! A dog would be good for Glenn."

"Good for *you* when you need a friend to keep you company outside, walking Dinah." She leaned down to stroke Dinah's muzzle and slip her another biscuit.

Pearl told me that she preferred a female cocker to a male— "none of that lifting of the legs!"—and that they were especially affectionate, though more prone to accidents than the males.

"There aren't going to be any accidents," protested Joe, "because crate training is almost foolproof as long as you keep taking the dog outside."

"Mmmmm. We'll see," sniffed Pearl slyly, assuring me that nothing was foolproof "except my cake," putting an extra piece of it in tinfoil for me. She ended our first little visit by saying, "Come by anytime."

CHAPTER THREE

The Runt of the Litter

Now I was getting excited.

It was all planned out in my mind.

If I got a dog in late summer or early fall, I'd have enough time to easily train the puppy before the weather turned cold, brutally so in Battery Park City, where the wind would howl around the corner of our building.

"Listen, friend, you don't want to be walking a puppy trying to figure out its head from its tail in a blizzard in January," lectured Joe, who now called me on a daily basis to "dee-scuss," as he pronounced it, "the homecoming arrangements for your dog."

There would be no pet stores for me this time around. "You never do that," he admonished. "It's twice the money for half the quality, so either rescue a dog from a shelter or get a puppy from a private breeder."

I set to work, researched cocker breeders, and finally found a reputable one in New Jersey—though the entire idea still seemed pretty abstract to me. But things were about to get a lot more concrete.

On July 15, 1988, after a nine-week pregnancy, Sweet Sue, a

champion cocker spaniel who had been known on the dog show circuit for her elegant carriage, gave birth to six blond-haired puppies in Mount Laurel, New Jersey.

The breeders, Tom and Betty Campbell, who had earned a reputation for raising prize-winning cockers, were delighted with the new pups, at least most of them.

At six weeks old, the puppies were assessed for their show prospects. The breeders kept the best two on their twelve-acre farm, and three more found homes almost immediately. But the last of them, the woebegone runt of the litter, was left behind, unwanted.

That's where I came in. I had been on Tom Campbell's waiting list, hoping for the perfect dog all summer. So I was disappointed to know that the "best" of the puppies were already spoken for.

"Well, we do have one left," he told me on the phone, as if offering a consolation prize. "We've named her Twiggy—because her legs are kind of spindly and her body proportions are off. She's a skinny little thing."

"Oh, great," I thought.

"So," Tom continued, "she'll never be a show dog, but I think she's going to have an unusually beautiful face—very symmetrical—and a perfectly blond, even coat."

Twiggy, Tom explained, was also the smartest of the bunch—the first to mischievously figure out how to escape from the pen and steal treats from a cookie jar by knocking it off a low ledge and rolling it over with her paws.

"That dog has something special about her," he chuckled. "Interested?"

I certainly was intrigued. And just as Pearl was about to change my life, so was this unwanted little creature named Twiggy.

As for the puppy's imperfections, I really didn't care. After all, I had no intention of breeding a dog or having one compete in dog shows. The only thing I wanted was an affectionate, healthy, cute puppy with a calm temperament.

"Okay Tom, I'd love to meet her. Assuming we click, I'll take her."

Over the next few days, I was consumed with getting prepared, determined to avoid any more faux-paws.

I wondered how the prospective puppy would adjust. This puppy was going from "Green Acres" to high-rise living. From day one, she'd be entering a world quite different than the one she knew on "the farm" in Jersey. We have a lot of greenery in Battery Park City, but no pastures or barns.

Upon her arrival, she'd be coming into a circular driveway that leads into an all-glass-enclosed lobby, allowing you to see straight through to the Hudson River and New Jersey coast. The circular doors spin busily morning and night with baby carriages, luggage carts, and dogs moving in and out.

Once inside, the pup would be traipsing past our doormen, Felipe and Dave, and into a long mirrored lobby with couches, armchairs, and a mural of the Hudson River, which leads toward a bank of four elevators.

Getting off on the third floor, she'd then trot all the way down to the very south end of a long red-carpeted hallway where she'd find the white door leading into my apartment.

Entering, the new puppy would see a kitchen, a long living room facing onto the marina, and a bedroom with an exposure facing west, directly onto the Hudson, with a view of the Statue of Liberty. The Esplanade, dog run, and the river were less than a five-minute walk away.

Not a bad setup for a city dog.

My focus was on the kitchen, which I'd outfitted with all the paraphernalia necessary for a puppy, as if I were turning it into a nursery for a newborn. Key were the baby fence enclosing the room and the metal kennel—big enough to allow the puppy to stand, stretch, and sleep, with adequate room to turn around.

I put cushiony pillows on its floor and a green towel on top to semi-enclose it and make it cozy. Also ready to go were the food and water bowls, puppy chow, assorted toys, and nylon bones for teething—all of it meant to give my puppy the perfect housewarming.

So on an overcast day in October, when Twiggy was twelve weeks old, the breeder Tom drove the remaining pup into Lower Manhattan for her "interview." I wanted all the support and help I could get that day, and felt lucky when Joe, and his partner Robert, offered to drive me over to the meeting place. "You're not going to want to take the puppy home in a taxi, all alone," said Joe, considerately.

So with Dinah at Robert's feet, we all piled into Joe's little white Volkswagen convertible for this early-fall adventure.

When we got over to our rendezvous spot—a parking lot near the South Street Seaport on Manhattan's East River—there was Tom standing outside a dark green van, the back hood up, with a beat-up dog crate near the opening.

"Finally, we meet," exclaimed Tom, a sturdy-looking man in his early sixties who put out his hand in welcome as he brought us around to the back of the car for a look at the star attraction.

And there in the crate sat poor Twiggy, a bedraggled blond ball of fur. She was shivering and raggedy. Her big brown eyes gazed up at us apprehensively.

"She's a little homely at the moment," apologized Tom, a master of understatement, "but she'll improve."

I wasn't convinced. The ragamuffin puppy had a scroungy, rough-around-the-edges look to her, with an overgrown, matted coat and freckles around her nose. I thought she was the doggie version of the 1950s blond cartoon character Pitiful Pearl. Most amusing, she hadn't yet grown into her ears, which were comically hanging halfway down her body. And did I mention that she was slightly bowlegged?

"Twiggy," Tom explained, "got a little carsick coming over here—so she threw up." Oh, great.

"It's not unusual for puppies," he assured me. "It's the first time she's ever been outside the farm, so she's a little out of sorts."

Twiggy drew back a bit and lay down, snuggling on what Tom described as her security blanket, a ripped pink cotton wrap "that has her mom's scent on it. Keep this with her for now. She really loves it and it reminds her of Sweet Sue."

Nearby were her two favorite toys, he said—a yellow plastic Scooby-Doo dog that made a squeaking sound and a long red snake that she clutched to her tummy.

Tom then opened the door of the kennel, slowly scooped Twiggy up, and gently put her in my arms.

This was the make-or-break moment I was waiting for.

"Well, hello there, little baby puppy," I whispered, as Twiggy curled into a ball, leaning against my chest. I held her close and discovered that she had the most delicious smell. I felt an immediate click. I really did. She was so warm, trusting, and sweet. The sensation of her leaning into me was indescribable. When she licked my face, that was pretty much it!

I had found my dog, the one I'd been waiting for, and I felt it with total conviction. I handed Tom a check, he wished me good luck, and off we went in Joe's VW, back down the FDR Drive to Battery Park City.

True, it had taken thirty-five years to accomplish this, but after my early fear of Strippy, the false start with Baby, and my test-dog, Dinah, at last I had found a dog of my own.

"I have an announcement to make, guys," I told Robert and Joe. "I *hate* the name Twiggy." Everybody laughed.

"It does conjure up a slightly pathetic image, doesn't it?" said Robert.

"So," I continued, "I'd like to introduce you to my new puppy. Her name is Katie."

"Well, that's an improvement," replied Joe.

I had decided to name my dog after my all-time favorite movie star—Katharine Hepburn.

A few years earlier, in the course of my work interviewing celebrities, I went to Miss Hepburn's house for a ham-and-cheese sandwich and a long talk. It was an unforgettable afternoon. The dazzle of this legend's presence—her incisive energy, wit, and intimidating hauteur as the grandest American actress of them all—left an indelible mark on me, as you'll later read.

I figured that maybe this little puppy from New Jersey, the runt daughter of Sweet Sue, could one day make a little magic of her own—and might even meet her namesake.

Katie snuggled contentedly in my arms on the car ride home, tuckered out and sleeping soundly.

CHAPTER FOUR

From Bow to Wow

When I got home, with Joe, Robert, and Dinah in tow, I carried Katie out of the car. The neighbors in the lobby oohed and aahed at the new blond puppy.

Katie was limp in my arms half-asleep, wrapped in her pink blanket, with her head resting sideways. That exhausted pup would have slept through anything.

"Who could *this* be?!" asked Nancy, my animal-loving neighbor whom I'd nicknamed "Bird Lady." Perched on her shoulder, as always, was the resplendent Mojo—a stunning red-and-blue greenwing macaw who knew how to talk.

"Pretty girl, pretty girl—want some chicken?!" crowed the bird, eyeing Katie by poking his head around Nancy's shoulder, his beak jutting forward. Katie half-opened one curious eye, then lazily closed it again, having had enough stimulation for one day. In due time, she'd recognize and come alive at the word *chicken*.

Entering my apartment, we went right into the kitchen, and just as Joe had predicted, Katie viewed the cushiony kennel as a welcome retreat. As soon as I bent down with her in my arms, she climbed right into it, sniffing her new blanket and cushions and pushing them all around with her paws, arranging everything to her liking. She then positioned her head on a blue pillow and fell soundly asleep, her two favorite toys placed next to her. She was home.

After a while, Joe suggested that we leave the room, giving Katie a chance to acclimate. But a minute after we'd disappeared into the living room, Katie started whimpering, then howling. It was pathetic. She was, after all, just a baby.

As I began heading back into the kitchen to comfort her, Joe stopped me. "No. No! You've got to let them howl. You need to teach them a lesson right from the start."

You *do*?

"Leave her alone and let her get used to it. Otherwise, she's always going to be a crybaby whenever you go away."

To me, Joe's advice seemed harsh, especially on day one, when Katie was disoriented and, no doubt, insecure without Sweet Sue or the farm environment to comfort her. I had no intention of following Joe's advice, though I pretended to.

I thanked Joe and Robert profusely for everything they'd done for me that day. And as soon as the door closed, I ran back into the kitchen, opened up the kennel door, and lifted Katie out of it, holding her snugly against me.

I had to show her off and couldn't wait another minute to introduce her to my neighbors Pearl and Arthur. I headed right down the corridor to 3C.

"Ohhhh, a special delivery!" Pearl cried, as she opened the door, entranced with the little pup. After we sat down at her dining table, I lifted Katie up and passed her over to Pearl, who cradled her in her arms. She started rocking her like a baby—and Katie was limply compliant and completely at ease, enjoying the attention.

"Oh, she's beautiful, just like when Brandy was a baby,"

cooed Pearl, stroking Katie's head and leaning down to kiss it, whispering sweet nothings.

"Hey, let me get a look at that little girl," said Arthur, walking out of the bedroom and eagerly sitting down to join us.

Katie perked her head up and then wriggled out of Pearl's arms, taking a walk on *top* of the dining table (Joe would have had a conniption) and climbing into Arthur's arms, licking his face. It was instant infatuation.

Katie then fell sound asleep in Arthur's arms, her paws wrapped over his wrists, softly snoring. As I watched this scene unfold, with all of us sitting around the table making small talk and enjoying the moment, I felt at peace, so incredibly calm.

Unlike the panicky sensation I'd experienced with Baby's arrival, I didn't feel alone at all this time around, thanks to Joe and my new friends down the hall.

That first night, I moved Katie's kennel into my bedroom so she could smell and feel my presence. And just before going to sleep, I looked down into the crate. There she was, irresistibly cute, stretched out on her back, looking up at me, teething contentedly on a nylon bone. At that moment, my heart just filled up with love and a deep sense of protectiveness for this little puppy. It was an intense feeling that I hadn't expected. I was just like any new parent—utterly entranced by the wonder of it all.

❧

Over the next few weeks, the smallest things about taking care of Katie gave me pleasure. I'd fill up her miniature water bowl (decorated with a picture of Minnie Mouse on the bottom of it), and she'd greedily drink from it, her tongue splattering water all over the floor.

She flew into her food bowl with gusto, and her nose and face were covered with mush by the time she finished eating. She'd try to sneeze it off—or tolerate my wiping her face clean with a paper towel, closing her eyes patiently. She'd then lick my nose a few times before hightailing it back into her pen, rolling on her back, and exposing her tummy in surrender, as if to say, *"Thanks Dad, gotta relax."*

In these euphoric puppy days, there were a series of "firsts" in store for Katie, as she was about to meet her doctor, her groomer, her trainer, my longtime housekeeper—and the ground outside.

That first morning, when I took her out, she looked perplexed at the alien cement, sniffing it suspiciously, wondering how it had replaced the grass she was accustomed to. She quickly turned toward the door, attempting to escape back into the building. *"C'mon, I don't like it out here,"* she seemed to say. But I held steady. And although she eventually did relieve herself, it took nearly a half hour to get the job done, a situation that worried me.

That morning, I made a beeline to a vet I'd found in Manhattan's Chelsea area, Dr. Scott Simon. He was super-tall, in his mid-thirties, with blond curly hair, a resounding voice, and a down-home demeanor. I had heard that he was meticulous in his exams. "So this is little Katie," Dr. Simon said, gently examining her from head to toe, paying special attention to her eyes and ears, which, in cockers, are susceptible to infection.

Katie tried to wriggle back into my arms, uncertain of this giant. "Just hold her steady, by the shoulders," he advised, as he carefully peered into her ears.

"Ahhh, I see that Katie has ear mites—nothing serious— just a few parasites from the farm. We'll get rid of those fast enough. And in five months or so, we'll spay her." He explained that the procedure reduced the chance of breast cancer and other tumors and infections, while spayed females also tended to have more even temperaments.

"No babies for Katie?" I asked.

"It's up to you—but I don't think you need to do that." I agreed with him, changing the subject to housebreaking.

"This morning," I told him, "Katie wasn't very interested in doing her business outside—and I need to know the best way to get her housebroken." Katie was lying down on the steel exam table, head over the side of it, sniffing for treats, and bored.

I explained that the breeder had suggested to me that the quickest way to housetrain a puppy was to use a baby suppository! "He told me that it glides right in—acting as a prompt to getting instant results—and that after a few days, the dog never needs it again."

"We sometimes do that for senior dogs," replied Dr. Simon, laughing, "but it can work for a puppy too—and it's not going to hurt Katie."

It sounded weird to me, and I wasn't crazy about administering this back-ended remedy, but I tried it the next day. For a second there, as I slipped it in, Katie looked indignant. Her eyes widened as she turned her head back around—as if to say, *"What's going on back there?"*—but it worked like a charm. After two days of this, Katie got the hang of it and never looked back, so to speak, again. No further proctological ministrations were required.

On the way out of the vet's office that first day, Dr. Simon had one final piece of advice: "Katie could use a good bath and grooming."

Indeed, at twelve weeks, Katie, more than most puppies, was definitely going through her "awkward" stage, like a gangly teenager. Her body proportions were all off, especially her long legs, which gave her an up-on-stilts look, making her slightly uncoordinated.

The vet explained that puppies are growing so rapidly their

heads and bodies part company, each developing at different rates. "So puppies don't often look their best until six or eight months. In the meantime, take this," he said, handing me a card for De De's Dogarama. "One of the best."

Heading down Seventh Avenue to Greenwich Village, we walked into this tiny emporium of beauty for dogs, outfitted with floor-to-ceiling kennels along the back walls, each filled with pampered mutts of every shape and size waiting for their shampoos, crème rinses, haircuts, pedicures, and manicures. With all the bathing going on, the room was as humid as a rain forest.

And there on the grooming table was a white standard poodle, standing obediently still as her elaborate coiffure was blown out to comic perfection. Presiding over it all was the young owner, a blonde named De De, happy to meet her new client.

For Katie, De De recommended a groomer named Betty, "a magician with puppies," she said. Betty was a tomboyish young woman with overalls, a short red pixie haircut, and tortoiseshell glasses. Dog hair covered her from head to toe. (Truthfully, she needed a good grooming as badly as Katie.)

Betty was bubbly and talkative, carrying on nonstop conversations with all her canine clients as she cut and trimmed. The dogs seemed to follow Betty's repartee with their eyes, lifting their paws when directed to.

"Hey Sport," Betty grinned, plucking Katie from my arms and burying her with a hug. "Oh, my my my," she surmised, "this little girl needs a makeover bad. Leave her with me and come back in three hours—no, make it three-and-a-half."

I hesitated, not wanting to leave Katie alone, but I was practically shoved out the door by the assertive De De. "No clients stay."

As I looked back, Katie was nose-to-nose with Betty, as the groomer chatted away to her. "Now look here, sister," she said, "you're a pup who needs a lot of help. Mama's going to give you the look you deserve."

When I returned, I did a double take. Standing on the counter, literally posing, was a blown-dried stunner who had gone from bow to wow.

Katie was literally unrecognizable with a pink satin bow tied daintily around her neck. Her hair was sleekly cut close to the body and looked slightly bleached and evenly blond. Betty had left an amusing fringe, like eyebrows, above her eyes, like a silent-era film star. Katie held her head high with a sense of hauteur, still as a statue as she showed off her new look. Her hair was so perfect that she almost looked like a stuffed animal. Her wagging tail told me that she'd thoroughly enjoyed the pampering.

As I was about to pick her up from the counter, Betty came up behind me, spraying a mist of something in our direction. "It's a nice parfum for dogs that we use," she said.

"Yeah," added De De matter-of-factly, ready to make a sale. "It's a floral bouquet with a soft powder-and-vanilla background, perfect for females," though I never did buy it (or want it used again), instead preferring the clean, fresh smell of just the shampoo.

Betty planted a parting kiss on Katie's wet nose — "see you next time, sister!" — and off we went.

There wasn't one person on the street who didn't turn around or stop us, as Katie was now irresistible.

CHAPTER FIVE

"Lion" in a Cage

Despite the grooming, within a few weeks of Katie's arrival, my apartment smelled "doggy"—a combination of puppy chow, her not-so-clean fur, and the accidents in the kitchen. And with Katie's toys and dog equipment strewn all over the place, it felt as if my entire existence had been thrown up into the air, in a happy way.

Although I tried, at first, to keep Katie in her crate next to me at night, she refused, and would cry unless I took her out of it and placed her on the bed.

I kept this a secret from Joe, who totally disapproved of dogs in beds, while I found my puppy's ability to burrow into the perfect warm spot quite entertaining.

She'd poke her head under the blanket and travel south, face down, heading toward my feet, finally resting her head on my toes.

During the night, she'd gradually make her way north again and lean against my side, my own little heating blanket. And by morning, her head was on my pillow, her long ears tangled around her face.

In her daytime hours, one of Katie's favorite recreations

was the sock game, the reason for all my mismatched socks. She'd pick one up from the floor and spit out half of it for me. I'd hold one end, she the other, and what ensued was a vicious tug-of-war. She'd growl and shake her head and pull on that poor sock until it was in shreds.

Sometimes I let her win, and she'd pounce on it, triumphantly trotting into the other room with it. She'd shake her head back and forth as if she'd caught some delicious prey. But when I won and pulled it out of her mouth, those eyes never left me until I threw it across the room again. I bought plenty of socks.

Within a week, I was so consumed with puppy care that my apartment was in complete disarray, so it was definitely time to have the place cleaned.

So the next "first" on our list was introducing my puppy to Ramon, my longtime housekeeper, who was also one of my best friends and confidantes, an energetic, incredibly optimistic person who always buoyed my spirits.

Ramon arrived every Tuesday morning and was horrified that first week, when he found Katie loose in the kitchen, energetically jumping up on the gate to greet him. He was terrified of dogs. Months earlier, when I had just mentioned the possibility of getting a dog, the ordinarily congenial Ramon turned stony. "I hate them," he said matter-of-factly, "and if you get one, I'll quit."

But I had defied his warning. I'll never forget that first Tuesday morning when he looked into Katie's pen and said, "Forget it!" He started to pick up his things and leave. I begged Ramon to stay. "I promise that she's harmless, and I'll keep her in the kennel with the door closed. She won't bother you at all."

Ramon slowly considered my offer, peering into the cage as

if he were looking at a wild lion. "Okay," he told me grudgingly, "we'll try it. But I don't think so."

Over the next few months, Katie worked on him, demonstrating how cuddly she could be, lying tenderly in my arms, seductively passive, or turning over on her back. The more Ramon resisted her advances, the more she tried to shake hands with him, throwing her paws in his direction, sometimes both at one time.

Katie knew what she was doing, sensing Ramon's fear and moving to melt it. It wasn't long before Katie was out of the cage and allowed to walk around, following Ramon as he worked. This was amazing progress.

One day, Ramon even ventured to pet Katie, and she licked his hand in return. He pulled it away, disgusted. "Yuck!" I could tell she was growing on him—but it was going to take a little longer for him to adjust.

In the meantime, I had to make sure that Katie was well on her way to being housebroken. Although as a puppy she was endlessly curious, she was also eminently trainable—at the perfect age to master city-style living.

For starters, she needed to be certain that relieving herself was an *outdoor* activity. To accomplish this, I took her out every two or three hours. I was determined to train Katie as quickly as possible because I had wall-to-wall carpeting throughout my apartment, the only washable floor space being in the kitchen.

In the morning, I'd scoop her up right out of the kennel and off we went—so she never had a chance for an accident. But by the afternoon, of course, it was inevitable that accidents would appear in the kitchen, most of them on the newspaper spread all around her kennel.

So for now, that room remained Katie headquarters. "I'm

not going *in* there," Ramon warned me. "And she's not coming *out* here."

Indeed, the baby gate barricaded Katie in, though it wasn't foolproof and didn't always stop her. As Tom had warned me, she'd been the first of the litter to escape the kennel.

So during her first week, I found the gate on the floor twice, with Katie lounging in the living room under a coffee table, casually chewing her bone. Another time, I found her sound asleep on a velvet pillow.

I then bought a stronger, higher gate. Most of the time, though, Katie had no reason to attempt a getaway, as I was usually home, in and out of the kitchen, and had her up and outside all the time.

And as Joe had predicted, Katie never had an accident *inside* her kennel, except once when she was sick. On that day, as I cleaned out her little house, she stood hovering close by, poking her nose around my arm, possessive of her territory and curious to supervise my invasion of it. And just as soon as I had finished fluffing up the freshly laundered blankets and pillows, she jumped back in, snugly content.

Beyond housebreaking, the next step was teaching Katie basic commands. As I knew nothing about obedience training, I hired a young man named Jonathan Klopp, an accountant-turned-trainer in horn-rimmed glasses who promised he'd whip Katie into shape within five easy lessons at fifty dollars an hour.

"Now the first thing we're going to do," he explained, "is teach Katie to *sit* whenever you want her to." As a reward and prompt, he recommended using Velveeta cheese "because puppies love it and it works perfectly."

He demonstrated this by putting his left hand out and gently pressing down on Katie's back, as he emphatically said,

"Sit," which she immediately did, hungrily eyeing that piece of cheese in his right hand. Jonathan popped the orange treat into her mouth every time she complied.

"Goooood girl!" he exclaimed, reinforcing good behavior with his tone of voice and the cheese, and then showing me how to do it too. Within a few minutes, Katie had "Sit" down cold—an expert.

A few days into practicing this, touching her back wasn't even necessary. With simply a finger motion in the down direction together with the verbal prompt, Katie sat like a little soldier, waiting for a treat, her brown eyes intently focused on the cheese. Gradually, we weaned her away from the cheese and she sat anyway.

Next, we worked on "Stay" and "Come," using the long red-carpeted hallway outside my door—a perfect "backyard" for fetching, running, and playing. Soon enough, with Jonathan holding a mouthwatering piece of that gooey cheese, Katie was racing down that corridor at the command "Come," triumphantly retrieving the treat. "Goooood girl!!" we'd both shout.

Katie became especially adept at "Shake," one of her favorite commands. At first, she'd hesitantly lift up her right paw, then the left, but once she got the hang of it, all you had to do was tempt her with a cookie and she furiously offered both paws—back and forth, like playing patty cake—until she got what she wanted.

Finally, and most difficult, was differentiating "Sit" from "Down," in which case Katie had to drop to the ground into a crouch, keeping her head flat on the carpet and not moving until told to. But after just a few weeks of practicing and keeping the refrigerator stocked with cheese, Katie had mastered it all—that is, until we went downstairs for a real-life test-drive.

So confident was I that she would obey me that we tried a walk inside the lobby *without* a leash. When a tenant opened the front door of the building, Katie slipped through it, gone in a flash. She raced outside like a jackrabbit, escaping at a blindingly fast speed, running across the circular driveway—where a car could have killed her. Then, she took off through the adjoining garden.

Naively, I hadn't expected such a surge of energy from a puppy so small.

"Katie, Katie! Come!" I furiously hollered. She totally ignored me. No cheese—no results. I chased her down quickly, scooped her up and took her home, expressing my displeasure at her disobedience.

But she had a mischievous grin on her face, her tongue hanging out in pleasure as her little body heaved with the exertion. She was most pleased with herself.

Like any toddler, Katie was going through "the terrible twos." If she didn't have her favorite bone to chew, my sneaker sufficed. Shoelaces were fun too. And a black knit hat made a nice lunch. Her big brown eyes missed nothing.

One day, after grocery shopping, I left a sealed box of snack bars unattended for a few minutes as I went down to the laundry room. When I returned, all the green plastic wrappers had been neatly removed from each half-eaten bar, and Katie's face was covered in granola.

"What did I tell you about ya manners?" I'd exclaim, a common refrain over the next years. She'd look up at me, that pert black nose pointed in the air, tail down, then trot away, disenchanted with my tone.

One night, my decorator friend, Michael, came over for a spaghetti dinner. As he was sitting in the living room balancing a plate on his lap, Katie eyed it with great interest. When

Michael, who always had a great sense of propriety, looked away for a moment, Katie pounced, diving into his pasta headfirst.

"No, no, no!" I shouted, pulling her by her red collar away from the plate. She was licking her chops with pleasure at the caper, her entire face stained with tomato sauce.

Michael looked horrified. "She's completely out of control," he snapped.

I poured her briskly back into the kennel, though I admit to remarking that she did look kind of cute in her stained state. (We scrapped the spaghetti and went out to dinner—my treat.)

"I told you this would happen if you handed her the moon and the stars," clipped Joe the following day, satisfied that Dinah would never err on this side of danger.

"You've got to discipline that dog of yours," he warned, though I had no intention of ever hitting Katie or frightening her, instead preferring the slow, steady, firm approach. So I used lots of no's and Velveeta cheese, while secretly enjoying Katie's puppy pranks.

Once Katie was housebroken, she had full access to her extended "crib." This meant my entire apartment, including the newly renovated living room, a cozy space with red-striped wallpaper, ivory carpeting with a diagonal pattern of pale green vines on it—and lots of dog-comfy chintz.

With so many pieces of upholstered furniture to choose from, Katie discovered lots of soft places to snooze, observe, and hide.

Her favorite was a green tufted chair, and she'd often fall asleep on it, her head hanging down off it as she softly snored. Off-limits was the white silk couch, and she knew it, though it didn't stop her from trying.

"Katie, NO!" I'd exclaim, as I found her dozing on it more than once. And, with a knowing guilty expression, she'd leap quickly off it, her tail down.

Sometimes when the sun was streaming in, I'd find her on the carpet by the window, stretched out on her back, legs spread, as if sunbathing. Other times, she was lazily stretched out on the cool surface of the hallway floor.

Sometimes, I couldn't find her at all, until I looked closely.

Then, as I scoured the room, there she was, hilariously, burrowed under the table skirt, with only her black nose sticking out from underneath. This became a regular game. I'd say, "Katie! Where *are* you?" No movement. Finally, "Katie...I bet you're real *hungry*?!"

And like a rocket, she'd fly out from under the table, tail wagging, bound into the kitchen, then eagerly sit down on the floor, waiting for a treat.

When company came over, to keep a better eye on the proceedings, she'd trot into the living room and lounge under the black Chinese coffee table, biting on one of her bones. When it was all chewed up and gone, she'd trail into the kitchen and start scratching on the cabinet door that held the new ones.

Katie soon learned where just about everything was.

I'd ask her, quite softly, "Want to go OUT?" And in one long leap, she was off the bed, running toward the door. She'd pull the leash off the knob, sit down waiting to be hitched up, then race down the hallway to the elevator and patiently wait for it to open.

Smart and agile as she was, her physical abilities couldn't always keep up with her determined spirit. Most frustrating to her was her inability to leap onto the bed without my help, though she'd try. She'd make a running start but repeatedly fall short of the bed, falling back down onto the carpet like a failed gymnast, toppling over on her back, looking startled and confused.

But we worked it out. I'd say "go," she'd take a leap, and then from behind, I'd give her a big boost with my palms, lifting her onto the bed. Within eight months, she'd mastered the move. In fact, she was well on her way to running my entire household single-pawedly.

Now it was time to put her to work.

CHAPTER SIX

News Hound

I n the fall of 1988, as Katie was practicing her sitting, coming, and staying, and racing up and down the hall with her favorite blue rubber ball, I was busily looking for a full-time job as an entertainment reporter—hoping to end the isolation of working at home.

One wintry day in mid-November, I had a job interview set up at CNN and impulsively decided to take Katie along with me, as Pearl was away that day and I didn't want to leave her alone. Besides, I thought having a puppy present might break the ice.

"Wow," said the producer, Scott Leon, marveling at Katie's long ears. "She looks like Lady from *Lady and the Tramp*." I'd never thought of that, but she really did. "I bet she's photogenic." Katie shook her ears and went obediently "down" for a nap, snoozing under Scott's desk as we talked.

We had an enjoyable interview, but Scott must have ultimately thought the dog was better on-camera than me, because I didn't get the job. But it gave me a good idea.

From then on, I'd take Katie to *all* my interviews. It couldn't hurt. And with the weather getting colder, why not increase the entertainment value by dressing her up, usually military-style, in a navy-blue knit coat with brass buttons on it (sometimes complemented by a red knitted hat that tied under her chin in a bow).

Every time we went out on such appointments, Katie jumped into the back seat of the taxi and sat up with her paws on the door and her nose pressed up against the window, studying the view. She soon learned how to negotiate escalators, elevators, revolving doors, and subway steps, all while practicing her new manners.

One day later that month, I had an interview with Gil Spencer, the charismatic editor in chief of the *New York Daily News*. He had a great sarcastic wit and the ability to tease out someone's true personality. I instantly clicked with him. And he liked dogs too.

"Where did Katie go to journalism school?" he inquired, looking over my interview clips.

"Well, she took her undergrad degree from Columbia, her master's from NYU, and now she's ready to work," I joked. (Neither of those schools were in my résumé, as my degrees were in classical music, not journalism.)

I had three more follow-up interviews at the *Daily News*'s classic Art Deco headquarters on 42nd Street, an impressive structure that inspired the design of the *Daily Planet* building for all the Superman movies of the 1970s and 1980s.

I'd found after my first visit that dogs weren't allowed in the building—much less in the newsroom. But defying this rule, I snuck Katie in anyway, each time hiding her in a large shopping bag as we passed by the giant globe of the world slowly rotating in the lobby.

Only Katie's black nose stuck out from the bag as I passed by security guards at the elevator. When she started squirming a bit, I headed her off, "Shhhhhh!"

When we reached the newsroom floor, she'd leap out of the bag and trot through the bustling newsroom and into Gil's spacious office again.

She'd sit on Gil's lap and work her magic on him, putting her paws on his desk as he scratched her ears. She never did lick his face, perhaps sensing that this was supposed to be business.

On the final visit, he sent me down the hall to meet the Sunday magazine editor, Jay Maeder, who was also a hospitable host to Katie. "I don't know how you got her in here, but she classes up the joint," he smirked. Well, at least they'd never forget this job applicant.

A few days later, I got the call that I was hired! I'd begin in January. And I credited Katie, in some measure, for using her canine charms to land me the job.

Over the next few weeks before I started my new full-time job in midtown, Katie began visiting her new friends Pearl and Arthur more often than ever.

It had all started one morning when I accidentally left my front door ajar after taking out the garbage. I went back into the bedroom for a few minutes, and when I returned to the kitchen, Katie was gone. She'd knocked down the baby gate and pushed open the front door to escape. When I went into the hallway, she wasn't there either.

I knocked on Pearl's door, and when it opened, there was my dog, sitting contentedly on Pearl's green-upholstered dining room chair, her paws gripping the tablecloth, busily eating a piece of toast right out of Arthur's hand. She didn't even turn around to look at me.

"How did this happen?!" I asked, as Pearl and Arthur laughed with uproarious delight.

"She's my girl now," Arthur said.

"Your dog," said Pearl, "has a mind of her own."

And from that time forward, every morning after eating breakfast and slobbering water all over the kitchen floor, Katie waited impatiently at my door, scratching the wall, anxious to get down the hall into her new friends' apartment.

Within a year, my doorway had to be replastered and repainted from all her scratching. I told my friends I was somewhat insulted that my own dog couldn't wait to get away from me. But there was no stopping her. It was as if she was telling me, *"Dad, I gotta get going. See ya!"*

Once we got the morning routine down, I didn't even have to leave my apartment. After her regular walk outside and breakfast, Katie would barrel down the red-carpeted hallway from my apartment and make a hard right turn into Pearl's, pushing against the door, which Pearl now left open. Katie would then trot over to the dining table and jump up on her hind legs to grab a piece of crispy toast, which was always waiting for her, from the corner of the table.

Then, in one smooth motion, she'd leap onto the dining chair and daintily arrange her paws on the table, waiting for some French toast or a snippet of bacon.

"Girlie! You're hungry today," laughed Pearl.

"Don't bite!" scolded Arthur, torturing Katie by dangling a piece of bacon above her.

Gulp. Down it went.

Katie also acquired a taste for honeydew melon and apples, and would soon become an expert at eating corn on the cob (side to side without missing a kernel) and watermelon too (spitting out the seeds). After her various snacks, she'd cover Pearl's face with kisses, then trail into the bedroom, getting a boost up from Arthur to get on the bed. She'd snooze on Pearl's nightgown or watch TV for the rest of the morning.

Amazingly, Katie did have an inner alarm clock, and at exactly 5:00 p.m. each day, she'd go to her food bowl, sit down, and wait impatiently for either Pearl or me to fill it.

Then, later at night, she did everything in reverse, scratching at Pearl's doorway, anxious to go home to me. What a routine—from their bed to mine, from one food bowl to another—a perfect life for a dog.

And so it was that my new puppy had essentially two homes—and was determined to have equal access to both. And even though I never intended for Katie to become a permanent part of Pearl's household, our routine evolved naturally and became the catalyst for a budding friendship.

"Once you begin your job in January," said Pearl, "just leave her here in the morning and we'll take care of her until you get home."

"You WILL?" I asked incredulously, touched by this generosity. I had planned on hiring a dog walker, but since Katie was only five months old, I was worried about leaving her alone at home between walks.

But beyond the expediency of finding Katie babysitters, my friendship with Pearl and Arthur was touching my heart in ways I hadn't expected.

I had always loved the company of my grandparents (and older people in general)—and was especially close to my maternal grandmother, Essie, who lived in Buffalo, New York.

Nana, as we nicknamed Essie, was nearly ninety years old—but still clearheaded, charismatic, and a great conversationalist, my all-around favorite person in the world. When I was a kid, she was truly a second mother to me and to my sisters. I became jubilant whenever I saw her car pulling up into our driveway, her yellow tortoise-shell purse catching the light.

Sometimes we'd sit at the kitchen table, laughing for hours as Nana quizzed me on American history, afterward treating me to her fantastic crumb cake or signature Cream of Wheat.

She also played the piano—usually "The Skating Song," a popular tune in the silent movie days. But mostly, she'd sit on the bench next to me, encouraging my efforts at the keyboard (and years later, attending all my piano recitals).

When I was hospitalized in my twenties for a stomach ailment, there she was, nursing me back to health; a few years later, when my first book was published, she was next to me at Barnes & Noble, smartly dressed, as I signed copies.

And five years after that, we marketed Nana's shortbread meringue cookies, dubbed "Essie's Crumby Dessert Squares... The Crumbiest You Ever Had." Katharine Hepburn, Peter Jennings, Nancy Reagan, Calvin Klein, and Paul Newman all raved about them, giving her endorsements. They were sold at Bloomingdale's and led to such newspaper headlines as "Top Stars Clamoring for More of Buffalo Grandma's Cookies" and "Cookies Turning a Grandmother into Rising Star." Nana was now being interviewed on television and signing autographs!

In short, Nana was remarkable in every way—and with me, every step of the way. On my first visit home with Katie for Thanksgiving, my dog sat on Nana's lap, looking up at her with adoration—and with high hopes, for she had the baker *herself* popping those delicious meringue squares into her mouth.

"She's nice and warm—a good blanket," laughed Nana, stroking Katie's head, and later sneaking her pieces of turkey under the table.

Nana was especially thrilled the day I called to announce that I'd gotten a full-time job at a newspaper. "Shhhhh. Don't tell anyone," she warned me, superstitious that good news could evaporate.

And now, on my phone calls home, Nana would listen, with relish, to all my stories about Pearl and Arthur and Katie's antics. "You tell Pearl I said hello!" Nana would always say.

With my grandmother still vital but slowing down physically and living in an assisted-living facility, I now, in a way, had "backup" surrogate grandparents right down the hall.

Their companionship and hospitality were therapeutic for me.

Likewise, I sensed that Katie and I were therapeutic for *them*—filling a void in Pearl and Arthur's lives. Arthur, an avid reader and TV watcher, didn't go out much as he was prone to respiratory infections and colds. And while Pearl busied herself with day-to-day domestic chores, she had more energy than she knew what to do with. Somehow, I sensed that both Arthur and Pearl were bored and a bit lonely in their retirement. After all, they had no children, and their dog, Brandy, was gone; they had few relatives, and the ones they had almost never visited.

I would later find out that Arthur had periodically suffered throughout his life from depression, though he seemed reasonably upbeat to me. In any case, having a puppy bounding around was definitely injecting new life into their household.

As for me, apartment 3C was fast becoming my safe harbor and Katie's favorite playpen—a place for relaxed conversation, sage advice, sharing neighborhood news, and relaxing with Katie. Thanks to Katie and Arthur and Pearl, the loneliness and isolation I had previously felt living alone were now gone.

"So you're sure you wouldn't mind?" I asked Arthur about leaving Katie in 3C all day.

"Mind?!" he laughed, pulling Katie against him in his favorite armchair. "I need this little toaster to keep me warm. I'm keeping her."

"The dog walker," added Pearl, always the practical one,

"can come by to get Katie at lunchtime and at five—but in between, she's ours."

Once I began the *News* job, I was consumed by it. Between writing Sunday magazine cover stories, a syndicated column called "Turning Point" about how celebrities recovered from crisis, and entertainment features for the daily pages, it seemed I was either at the office or away on day trips for interviews, practically never home. I had just about everyone you can imagine in my column, from film stars to criminals—sometimes one and the same.

Interviewing these people about their movies, shows, and books might have seemed glamorous—and it often was—but, for me, it was also incredibly stressful. Although I was usually at ease once the interview began, that first handshake was intimidating.

When the door opened, there was Meryl Streep, Elizabeth Taylor, Dolly Parton, Al Pacino, Diana Ross, Mia Farrow, Christopher Reeve, Sylvester Stallone, Bruce Willis, Calvin Klein, Carol Burnett, Mary Tyler Moore, Joan Kennedy, or Diane Sawyer—to name-drop just a few interview subjects from that first year. And that's not to mention one of my favorite repeat interviewees, Donald Trump. Tall, and intimidating at first, he turned warm and witty once relaxed behind his desk at Trump Tower for what turned out to be a series of long talks, first for the *Daily News*, then a multisession marathon interview for *Playboy*. This interview drew headlines due to his comments on Leona Helmsley and feelings about women and marriage.

Trump expressed his very human, more reflective side when expressing grief for the deaths of three of his executives in a helicopter crash and for the death of his older brother due to alcoholism. "I was very close to him and it was very sad when he died...toughest situation I've had."

When returning home from this kind of interview, I'd feel drained and content to return to my much less Trump-like existence, relieved to see Katie and Pearl and the gang, escaping what was, for me, a satisfying but stressful profession.

In hindsight, my work life felt a bit like *Fear Factor*. I pushed myself toward ever-more courageous (celebrity) stunts, and made a game out of how many "exclusives" I could pin down, while facing deadline pressure and my own anxiety about meeting celebrities.

That anxiety, however, often melted away when there was a genuine, heartfelt rapport between me and my interview subject. The most poignant example I can think of is a spring dinner at Senator Edward Kennedy's house, with all three of his children in attendance, the occasion being a Father's Day interview. "We never give anyone a house tour, but come on, let's take a look," the Senator told me, hospitably leading me into the enormous yellow-and-pink living room of his McLean, Virginia home, then later into his private study to reflect on the tragedies he'd endured. "Obviously, there's been a great deal of trauma, suffering, and loss in our family," he said, staring at the pictures of his brothers nearby on a table. "And it's been a heavy burden. My brothers were my dearest friends. They were just human beings—and wanted to be considered that way. I miss them," he finished, tears filling his eyes. "No day goes by when I don't. No way to bridge that."

At our farewell outside his house a few hours later, his advice to other fathers? "Let your children know you love them. That's what matters." And then the evening ended.

Times like these were, of course, exhilarating and moving, but more often than not, my associations with famous subjects continued to be a source of anxiety.

So while interviewing was good for my career, the pressure

of it wasn't always so good for me. And all of it was taking me further away from Katie. Although my dog was happy with Pearl and Arthur as her daytime keepers, I could tell she missed me.

Each night, when I finally got home, I'd knock on Pearl's door, and while waiting for her to open it, I'd get down on my knees on the carpet, ready to greet Katie at face level. The door would open, and Katie would practically leap out, flying into my arms, whimpering with a mixture of ecstasy and anxiety. *"Dad, you're home! I missed you,"* she seemed to be telling me, underlining my guilt at being absent for such a long stretch from morning to night.

In mid-March of that year, when Katie was eight months old, I took her back to the vet, Dr. Simon, to perform the spaying operation. I hated the idea of having my dog put to sleep for any reason and was anxious the entire day.

"She'll be fine, don't worry, go home, come back at six," Dr. Simon told me, shoving me toward the door just like De De always did. When I returned, Katie was lying down calmly inside the kennel, snoozing. As the door opened and she saw me, she ran into my arms as if we'd been separated a week.

Like any dog, she hated being alone. But unlike most high-rise city dogs, who do, by necessity, spend long periods of time alone—napping, bored and lonely, or being taken out for fifteen-minute walks by dog walkers and then promptly returned to their solitude—Katie was virtually *never* alone thanks to Pearl and Arthur.

In fact, my dog was a lot less lonely than I was. When I was on the road for business, there was nothing emptier than a hotel room. I hated it and missed the comfort of having Katie next to me at night. Sometimes when I'd call Pearl from Los Angeles, she'd put Katie "on the phone," and I'd talk to her.

Pearl would tell me that her tail would wag, though I doubt she got the "connection."

In short, like any working "parent," I had a real problem. I didn't know what to do about it until I decided to do the same thing *on* the job as I had done interviewing *for* jobs—take Katie along with me to work.

One or two days a week, I'd sneak Katie into the *Daily News* building via that shopping bag, and she'd snooze on a blue desk chair right next to mine, her head resting on the armrest, oblivious to anything or anyone. Puppies need their sleep. Most of the reporters liked seeing her around and came by to pet her, while a few grumbly ones resented her presence.

In fact, it wasn't long before the *New York Post*, our rival tabloid, ran this item in Richard Johnson's widely read column, PAGE SIX:

> *Daily News* writer Glenn Plaskin can't understand why his co-workers don't like his dog. Katie, a blond cocker spaniel that Plaskin occasionally brings to the office, has accompanied him on interviews with Leona Helmsley, Peter Jennings, and her namesake, Katharine Hepburn. Contrary to the story making the rounds in the newsroom, "Katie has never, ever relieved herself in the office," Plaskin told Page Six. "The fact is, she's better behaved than some of the people at the *News*."

Uh-oh! That item didn't make me too popular, though Katie did have her fans. One day, for example, the style editor dropped by and said she was writing a story titled "Fashion Goes to the Dogs."

"Would Katie like to model sweaters for us?" she asked.

Yes, she would!

As the story would explain, "pet clothing is going to be a tremendous fashion movement." Proving it, there was Katie in the cover photo, snuggled in the arms of a young female model, both of them in matching $250 beige-and-cream hand-knit wool sweaters.

"During a puppy's first winter," the story advised, "you should put on a sweater when the temperature is below 40." Katie was happy to do the job because she got a brand-new sweater out of the deal. And not long after that, *Family Circle* magazine invited her to model in a summer picnic pictorial, a huge platter of fried chicken nearby (most of it taken home by us in a doggy bag).

At these photo shoots, and at others to follow, Katie would typically be perched up on a raised white or clear pedestal, surrounded by bright lights and reflecting panels, obediently taking direction from the photographer and his assistant—none of it bothering her.

"Over here, Katie," the photographer would say, snapping his fingers and holding his hand up where he wanted her to focus. "Look straight ahead now"—and so she would, remaining perfectly still, staring straight at the camera, holding the pose. Then the assistant would go over to turn her head to a different angle, and she'd stay put.

True, I was sometimes behind the camera, holding up a biscuit, saying "Stay," but even when I didn't, she remained attentive, as if to say, "*Dad! This is fun. Don't bother me.*"

One time, when the shoot was over, she didn't want to get off the platform and kept climbing back up on it. Finally, she rolled on her back and spread her legs wide. The photographer noted, "We're not *that* kind of magazine!"

CHAPTER SEVEN

Prancing with the Stars

N ow that Katie was perfectly housebroken and had mastered all her commands, she was up and out of the house more than ever—Miss Sociable, parading in and out of our building with Pearl and Arthur, who now treated her as their very own dog. (Some of our neighbors thought Katie *was* their dog.)

But whenever I could wrest my dog away from her second parents, I had plans of my own.

To make my job more fun, I decided to defy Katie's critics at the *News* and to take her along with me on as many interviews as possible. And she was soon rubbing shoulders (and noses) with a host of celebrities.

In November 1989, for example, I had a long interview with Ivana Trump, then president of Manhattan's Plaza Hotel, which was, at the time, owned by her soon-to-be ex-husband Donald.

The tall, bubbly Ivana—glamorously outfitted in a hot pink suit and amethyst-and-diamond earrings—was more exquisitely groomed than any celebrity I've ever met.

Sitting in her Plaza Hotel office (not far from the gold-leafed Palm Court that she had meticulously restored to its lush glory), Ivana told me all about her bleak early years in Communist Czechoslovakia working at a shoe factory, bent over an assembly line.

As I wrote, "Ivana serenely gazes now at her custom-made silk pumps, and contemplates their continuing lesson, vowing 'that I was never—EVER—going to do that kind of work again.'" Indeed not.

I was taken by Ivana's infectious energy, self-discipline, and determination to prove herself as a businesswoman.

She was also an avid dog lover—and told me all about her beloved Choppy, a miniature black poodle who sometimes skidded across or slipped on the expansive marble floors at the fifty-room Trump Tower apartment where she and Donald lived.

A few weeks after our interview, when I stopped by the Plaza with Katie to say hello, Ivana swept into her office, threw her fur coat on a nearby chair, and beamed with delight. "So *this* is Kaaaaatie," she exclaimed. "What a beauty! Let me see." She effortlessly swept my one-year-old up in her arms and held her high in the air. (Katie looked none too pleased trying to defy gravity.)

"I have a meeting with our board of directors now," Ivana told me. But she was game for some fun. "Let me introduce her," and off Katie went in Ivana's arms, looking back at me curiously, as if to say, *"Who is this, Dad?!"*

A few minutes later, Katie was returned and Ivana departed, giving her a kiss good-bye. "Everyone loved her! She's the greatest."

At Christmas of that year, Ivana's secretary called, inquiring about the name of Katie's groomer. Figuring that Ivana liked Katie's haircut, I told her all about De De's Dogarama, though uptown dogs of Choppy's ilk were usually groomed at the much more exclusive Le Chien. It wasn't a day later that Katie got a wonderful Christmas present from Ivana in the mail, a gift certificate for a full year of grooming at De De's! Ivana was now the *greatest* in Katie's book.

That same year, I had an interview with Farrah Fawcett, who was then starring in a TV movie, playing the legendary *LIFE* magazine photographer Margaret Bourke-White. Over tea in the Bar Seine at Manhattan's Hôtel Plaza Athénée, we were talking quietly when Farrah's long-time companion, Ryan O'Neal, unexpectedly burst into the room. The chemistry between them was electric.

"Give me a kiss!" exclaimed Ryan, bending down toward Farrah as they passionately embraced, the actor almost stepping on poor Katie, who was sprawled out on the carpet chewing on a bone. "*Dad, he's bothering me*," she seemed to say, hightailing it under my chair. High-strung Ryan looked none too receptive to Katie either, though Farrah fussed over her.

"Isn't she adorable?" whispered Farrah in her distinctively buttery voice, music to a dog's ears. I supposed Ryan thought it odd that I had brought a dog to the hotel.

"So nice to meet a fellow blonde!" Farrah laughed, stroking Katie's ears. Farrah then took a sip of champagne and held hands with Ryan as the couple started chatting, speaking lovingly of the child they had had together, Redmond O'Neal.

When I asked them about their long-term (off and on again) relationship, which ultimately lasted almost thirty years, Ryan boomed, "Farrah and I have no plans to marry [they never did], neither do we have plans to separate." (They did separate in 1997, though they remained extremely close, and nearly did marry toward the end of Farrah's life in 2009 during the time before her death when she was being treated for cancer.)

"He's *always* wanted to marry me," Farrah added softly

that day once Ryan left the room, "from the first time we slept together. After we make love, he'll say, 'I'm not kidding you, you've *got* to marry me.'"

After our rather intimate talk, Farrah and I took Katie for a long walk up Park Avenue, onlookers fascinated as Katie, not yet set on her leash manners, kept pulling on it, at one point tangling up the former *Charlie's Angels* star, who was such a good sport. Sensitive and so down to earth, Farrah was a pleasure to talk to—and Katie gave her a big lick good-bye.

That same week, Katie met the renowned interior designer Mario Buatta, known as the "Prince of Chintz," the acknowledged master of the English country style that featured yards of swags, bows, and ruffles, plus lots of dog paintings.

Irreverent—despite such clients as the Forbeses, Barbara Bush, and Blair House (the president's guest house)—Buatta was notorious as a prankster. He once showed up at a Peggy Lee concert with a monkey on his lap, strolled through Central Park in an all-blue chintz suit, and arrived at a masked ball wearing a lamp shade on his head.

When I met him, he was rather tame in a dark blue suit, and just as funny as I expected. "My mom once told me," he said, "'maybe you'd like to be a psychiatrist or an actor or a lawyer'—but I combined all three and became an interior decorator!"

Months later, after we had become friends, Mario came over to my apartment one evening, bringing along as a present one of his signature dog pillows with a painted spaniel curled up on it. This was a gift for *me*, though Katie started ripping away the tissue paper as I took it from Mario's hand.

"This isn't for you!" Mario lectured Katie, who scrammed away, as she was never comfortable around tall people (Mario was over six feet tall). But this didn't stop Katie from requisitioning that pillow. When I wasn't looking, she knocked it off the couch and I found her napping on the carpet with it under her head. When he said good-bye, Mario commented that Katie's fur would make a nice glazed wall color.

That night, I discovered that Katie was doing a little redecorating of her own. She had pushed the pillow into her kennel and arranged it carefully with her paws. She napped on it nearly every afternoon thereafter.

Mario told me about a married couple who sold reasonably priced animal paintings out of a mobile truck. On his advice, I soon had hunting dogs, spaniels, and assorted other canines decorating my living room walls.

"Now you're English!" he joked.

In addition to such meet-and-greets with local interview subjects, I was also determined to take Katie with me on flights to Los Angeles. In past years, traveling on business always left me feeling incredibly depressed and disconnected from my routine, friends, and, of course, my dog. So I came up with a plan to permanently rid myself of loneliness on the road — take Katie along with me. It was the perfect solution, much better than Prozac.

But flying with a dog, even then, wasn't the easiest thing to do. And I had no intention of "checking" Katie in the luggage compartment — a requirement of most airlines unless you had a very small dog that could fit into a kennel placed under the seat. Otherwise, a dog like Katie, weighing twenty-eight pounds, was relegated to the cargo hold — subjected to possible changes in temperature and air pressure that could be fatal to a dog, not to mention the terror of being trapped for six hours in a cage, alone in the dark!

I had to avoid this. So I hatched an underhanded, though

pragmatic, plan. I persuaded our vet to write a letter stating that Katie was a "hearing dog," specially trained for the hearing-impaired and therefore allowed to travel freely through the airport and onto the plane.

It worked. So after being escorted through security, Katie would march through the airport in her hat and coat, arrive at the gate, and jump onto a chair in the waiting area, quickly inundated with admiring new fans. Stressed-out travelers practically lined up to pet her. Kids wanted to feed her snacks. Several people wanted to take her picture. A Marine stopped by and said it did his heart good to see a dog.

Sometimes she'd offer her right paw to "shake," fascinated by the stream of visitors. Other times, she was too busy to bother, chewing on a bone, not interested in making new friends, as if to say, "*Dad,... I'm busy... I can't talk to everybody!*"

Then we would board the plane. We were usually put in the bulkhead at the front, with Katie snoozing on the floor, though if there was no passenger next to me, she snuggled on the seat, sipping water out of a cup or eating a few nuts or potato chips. Anytime the flight attendants passed by, I was careful not to answer unless I was looking right at their lips. To Katie's credit, she never had an accident, not once.

In retrospect, I should never have billed Katie as a hearing dog, out of respect for hard-working service animals who alert their owners to fire alarms, knocks on the door, telephones, kitchen timers, or even prowlers. But I wanted Katie with me and was desperate to protect her from that cargo hold.

Once we got to the Beverly Hills Hotel (where I frequently stayed) and were taken into a bungalow behind the main building, Katie would prance around, poking her nose here and there. She would run outside into the lush gardens and savor the California sun like a true Hollywood hound.

On one memorable trip, I was to interview Bette Midler. The night before, we settled into bungalow 7A, one shaded by beautiful palms and a wild array of flowers and vines. Having Katie with me was like a tonic, erasing loneliness and anxiety. That night, even though Katie had been groomed a few weeks earlier, she looked a little rumpled, so I decided it would be fun to give her a bath, something I never did. What a mistake.

Katie winced when she got shampoo in her eyes, it took forever to rinse her off, and she slipped and slid all over the porcelain tub. I was surprised how much work it was handling her, not unlike a slippery watermelon. Finally, I was so soaked with water that I got into the tub, naked, not expecting the impact of those sharp nails from her paws. Ouch!

When Katie was finally all blown out and dried and fluffy, I opened the bungalow door ready to take her out for a walk, but she escaped in a flash. I went frantically looking for that naughty mutt everywhere along the winding pathways.

"Is this yours?" a man asked a few minutes later. And there, standing in the doorway of a nearby bungalow was the comedian Alan King, with Katie wrapped in his arms, a guilty look on her face.

"She looks familiar, but if you'd like to take her off my hands...."

He handed her over to me with his left hand, puffing on a cigar with his right. "Best offer I had all day," he laughed, closing the door.

❧

The next morning, we met the Divine Miss M in a suite at our hotel. Accustomed to seeing her in wildly extravagant stage costumes and elaborate makeup, I was taken aback by this understated, diminutive, rather serious-looking woman. She was dressed casually in black pants and a white sweater, wearing green-framed glasses and no makeup—so down to earth in every way—and delighted to see a *dog*, instead of just another probing journalist.

"This is going to be *different*," Bette exclaimed wryly, noticeably more interested in Katie than me. "My, my, my girlie, you're just adorable," she cooed, lifting Katie up by the front, her back paws hanging in midair. "How old is she?"

"Two—the terrible," I laughed, explaining her recent escape.

"Would you mind if I hold her in my lap?"

Not at all.

And for the next two hours, as Bette discussed her movies and the course of her life, Katie slept soundly on Miss M's lap, curled into a ball. One minute, Bette was serious, shy, and vulnerable, the next, funny, flirty, and sly.

"There are," she told me that day, "two people living in this body. I have a duchess and a tramp mentality. I love the low life and still have an affinity for it." Not so different from my mischievous dog. But through it all, Katie never moved.

Right up to the end, she remained asleep. "I can't believe this dog," said Bette, in parting. "She's so sweet, so calm. I've got to get one. Can you please give me the name of the breeder?"

Katie opened her sleepy eyes and reluctantly got off Bette's lap, wagging her tail, having made a new friend. (Gratefully, there were no accidents.)

❧

Katie got quite a different reception a few weeks later from Leona Helmsley, one of my favorite interview subjects, the hotel queen who had been dubbed by the press the "Queen of Mean."

I can tell you that she was never mean to me. (After we became friends, I told her about my grandmother, Nana, who was diagnosed with bone cancer in 1990 and was being treated in a Buffalo hospital. The next day, three dozen white roses were delivered to Nana, with a note signed "Love, Leona.")

Her legal problems aside, Helmsley had unbelievable charm and intelligence and I liked her immensely. After being introduced by the New York public relations legend Howard Rubenstein, we struck up an immediate rapport in both of our *Daily News* interviews and in an extended *Playboy* magazine interview.

As I wrote in *Playboy*, "Part brass-horn comedienne, Jewish mother and tragic heroine, Helmsley was soon pouring out her heart to me.... She was also quick with the solo one-liners. To wit: when Harry entered the breakfast room, zipping his pants: 'Don't brag, darling!'"

One hot summer day, I was having lunch with Leona and her husband Harry at their 200-acre Connecticut estate Dunnellen Hall, enjoying mushroom soup and a salmon fillet. I was telling them both all about Katie. Back then, Leona didn't yet own her beloved dog "Trouble," a white Maltese to whom she would later leave $12 million in her will.

"She sounds like a savvy dog...I'd like to meet her," Leona said gamely.

"Well, I guess not today," I told her. "Katie is back in Manhattan. Next time."

"Oh, no, no, darling," she insisted. "I want to meet her *today*. I'm going to send my driver to get her—*now*." She then picked up the phone, and instructed the chauffeur to pick up my dog thirty miles away.

"What's her address?" she asked.

I quickly telephoned Pearl, told her that a limo was coming for Katie, and asked her to put Katie into the car for the trip.

"Are you kidding?" Pearl gasped in disbelief.

"Pack her up!"

And so it was, just a few hours later, my dog arrived at the Helmsley estate in high style, her head poking out of the back window of a black Lincoln limousine, her ears blowing in the wind as the car pulled into a long tree-lined driveway and up to the gigantic portico.

As I opened the car door and scooped her into my arms, Leona came up to us, and looked her up and down, stroking her head. "She'd make a nice coat!"

Harry came out, tipped his cap to Katie, and offered to take us all for a ride on his electric golf cart. This was surreal.

In an instant, there I was, sitting next to Manhattan's legendary real estate billionaire, being driven around with the notorious Leona and my dog. When we got back to the house, I picked Katie up, intending for her to join us inside.

"Oh, no, darling," said Leona with a warning in her voice. "I don't want the marble floors scratched. Leave her in the car."

It must have been 90 degrees that day. "We'll leave on the air-conditioning," she offered.

Surveying the sculpted hedges, exquisite gardens, and manicured lawns, I wondered what would happen when Katie would eventually need to relieve herself. It didn't take me long to find out.

An hour later, when I was bidding farewell, we went outside and Katie was gone! She had jumped out of the open window of the limo and escaped into the vegetable patch, where she had relieved herself and was munching on something edible.

"What?!" exclaimed Leona, her face turning red. I feared I was about to see the dark side of the hotel queen. But then, a good sport, she smiled and had the car turned around.

"Time for you both to hit the road," she laughed, bidding Katie farewell.

I leave the best for last. My favorite interview subject of all time was the incomparable Katharine Hepburn, who had little need for publicists, instead setting up interviews at her East 49th Street townhouse *herself*, giving terse commands before hanging up the phone.

"Ham and cheese. Twelve-thirty."

Click.

Those were the instructions I always received when being invited over for lunch by "Madame," as Miss Hepburn was nicknamed by one lifelong friend.

Before and during my *Daily News* years, I interviewed Miss Hepburn many times (such as for her eightieth birthday, for her autobiography *Me*, and for a TV movie, *The Man Upstairs*, costarring Ryan O'Neal). But the pattern never varied and the menu never changed: homemade zucchini soup and melted ham and cheese, followed by something chocolate, which I usually brought along. (I'd often pick up her favorite dark chocolate "turtles" with pecans from Mondel Chocolates.)

One time, I presented her with a truly magnificent truffle cake, which I was looking forward to tasting. "Ah, fascinating," she uttered, looking into the box. "Norah!" she hollered down to her cook. "Come up and take this away."

Then, turning to me, she remarked, "It's much too good for lunch—I'll eat it for dinner!" and it disappeared into the kitchen.

That same day, I asked her whether she ever thought about death. "Death," she answered sweetly, "will be a great relief. No more *interviews*. Now pass the peanuts."

After eight years of knowing Madame, we became friendly

enough to chat off the record as well, so I occasionally went over to her townhouse for purely social lunches.

I also, from time to time, acted as a conduit, introducing her to people she was interested in, most notably Calvin Klein, whom I had previously interviewed for *Playboy*. The king of American fashion had, of course, met just about every celebrity in the world he'd ever wanted to—*almost* everyone, that is, except for Miss Hepburn. I felt honored to be able to bring these two legends together.

On the day of the lunch, Calvin came up the stairs into her drawing room holding in his arms exquisitely tailored wool and cashmere sweaters and pants, all wrapped in tissue paper, one-of-a-kind pieces he had made especially for her. He held them out to her as a gift.

In a teasing mood, she looked gamely at Calvin, at first not willing to accept them. Then, with her chin in the air, she teased, "Are they *free*?!"

"Of course they are," he smiled. She then handily lifted them out of his arms and disappeared upstairs into her bedroom to examine them. Later, the twosome sat side by side, engrossed in their discussion of fashion in the thirties and forties.

A few months after that stellar introduction, I figured I'd try another, which is where Katie came into the picture.

So one day, I asked Miss Hepburn, "Would you like to meet Peter Jennings?"

"Peter WHO?" she inquired, chin again jutting into the air. "Who *is* he?"

"You know, the ABC news anchor. He's on TV every night."

"Mmmm," she sniffed, "I don't watch the show. All right, bring him by."

Peter was a bit more thrilled about the upcoming lunch than Miss Hepburn, and promised to bring along, as a gift, what he described as his wife's incomparable brownies, pre-warned about Miss Hepburn's passion for chocolate.

The day of the lunch I decided to bring Katie along so Miss Hepburn could finally meet her namesake. But I only wanted Katie to stay for the introductions, not for lunch, as I knew my treat-hungry dog would be begging for food.

To manage the logistics, a friend of mine, Dean, came along in the car with Katie, me, and Peter. Dean would take Katie home after her cameo.

On the car ride up to East 49th Street in the Turtle Bay neighborhood, Katie sat snugly on Peter's lap, her paw on his arm, unimpressed with the legendary news anchor, but never taking her eyes off his foil-wrapped package of brownies.

"Katie, relax," admonished Peter, who was a dog lover and owned a Wheaten terrier named Bogart. "These aren't good for dogs," he told her in his distinctive baritone. Katie then took her right paw and slapped it against his arm, begging him, with no success.

Miss Hepburn greeted us outfitted, as always, in well-worn pants, a white turtleneck, red sweater, and a heavily frayed long-sleeved shirt.

I was surprised by how shy she seemed meeting Peter—maybe it was because he was someone outside her regular sphere. And Peter also seemed uncharacteristically reserved, almost as if this patrician actress intimidated him more than the legions of dictators he'd interviewed. As for Katie, she was oblivious to this exceptional company, her tail wagging as she ran up the wooden stairs into the drawing room, circled it once, and then lay down near the fireplace.

"Who's *this*?!" asked Hepburn, glaring down at Katie. My dog's tail immediately went down and she drew closer to the fireplace.

"I wanted you to meet my dog, Katie...."

"Mmmm. How'd you come up with that name?"

"I named her after you!"

"Small compliment. A midget me."

"Now," dismissing my dog with a look of total disinterest, "Mr. Jennings, we're having ham and cheese."

I felt really embarrassed, as this was the first and only time I'd ever brought Katie along to an interview when she bombed, so to speak. You can't win them all.

I scooped my dog up and handed her off to Dean, waiting outside. The rest of the lunch was uneventful, until dessert.

"Glenn told me how much you love chocolate, and these are the best, made by my wife," Peter said, handing over his offering.

"Let's have a bake-off," replied Miss Hepburn, all ready for this, as I had told her Peter was bringing brownies. "Norah!" she commanded, hollering down the staircase, "bring up the brownies."

Miss Hepburn then set one of Peter's brownies and one of her own side by side on a white china plate, munching into one at a time. After a moment of careful consideration, she proclaimed, *Mine are much better!*"

Peter was a great sport, laughing uproariously, promising not to relay that information to his wife.

And that was it for lunch. Peter had met a legend. Miss Hepburn had won the bake-off. And Katie had met her match.

CHAPTER EIGHT

Walter the Horse

Favorites and Foibles

The next four years flew by in a flash, a blur of celebrity interviews, trips to California (with my "hearing" dog in tow), and countless runs up and down our red-carpeted hallway.

Katie was now at her energetic best, practically defying gravity as she jumped and skipped behind me to Pearl's, carrying in her mouth chew bones, rattles, rubber balls, and a noisy pink rabbit—which she shook furiously from side to side in order to make it squeak.

Scratching at Pearl's door with her paws, Katie would drop her toys onto the carpet as precious offerings. She'd then try to slip craftily between Pearl's legs into the apartment for a snack. To tease her, Pearl would purposely block Katie from entering, as if playing soccer. The game would continue until Katie slinked around Pearl, her true goal being the dining table to snatch a piece of crispy toast, which she would then munch on loudly.

Although Katie loved being indoors, she also relished exploring our neighborhood. Often, as she was lazing on my bedspread, I'd ask, in a rather soft voice, "Want to go OUT?"

And in one long leap, she was off the bed, running toward the door. She'd pull the leash off the knob, sit down waiting to be hitched up, then race down the hallway to the elevator and patiently wait for it to open. In cold months, I'd ask, "Where's your COAT?!" And using her mouth, she'd pull a coat off a shelf and push it toward me.

As we came off the elevator, she'd expertly navigate from the front lobby door out to the Hudson River. First, trotting briskly through our garden on the way to the water, she'd typically spot a bird and twirl into the air attempting to catch it.

Likewise, when a brave squirrel climbed down a tree to snoop around the ground, Katie was on the hunt (proving her ancestry as a sporting dog), though she was never fast enough to catch the agile rodent, who would race back up the tree once she leapt in for the kill.

Katie would then continue on through the garden, pulling me forward toward the doormen in each of the buildings in our complex, anxious to say hello and retrieve a biscuit from them.

She'd then lead the way toward the ice-cream shop at the corner, hoping that I might buy a frozen treat, usually a pistachio cone that we would share. After polishing that off, she'd trot further west to the outdoor volleyball court that overlooked our marina and barge into the game by running around the court chasing the ball.

"Katie, no, you're in the way," I'd shout, apologizing for the intrusion, but she persisted, determined to meet new people and have some fun. *"Dad, I need some exercise—and this game is a good one!"*

To appease her desire to chase and retrieve, I'd usually have a tennis ball in my pocket and would pitch it into the air once we got to the nearby park. Like a major-league outfielder, Katie would carefully follow that ball with her eyes as she ran and leapt high into the air to catch it before it hit the ground. After she became breathless, I'd pour water into a cup for a long drink before we continued on.

Once out on the Esplanade, she walked briskly along the water's edge, sniffing under every bench, scouting for food, and, on hot summer days, searching for the perfect shady spot under an oak tree for a long nap.

At other times, Katie's ears pricked up when she heard the sound of hoofs hitting the pavement. That was the signal that our neighborhood's mounted policeman, Sean, was out on patrol, sitting high up on his magnificent Belgian quarter horse, Walter.

Walter, Sean told me, had been raised on a farm with dogs, so anytime we passed, the horse would stop and scoop down his head and affectionately rub noses with Katie, his wide nostrils quivering with pleasure.

Katie, in turn, would lick his face. Sometimes, I'd hoist Katie up to *him*—and she'd playfully swat him in the wide space between his eyes. The picture of this huge horse nuzzling a pint-sized spaniel was endearing beyond belief, heartwarming to all who saw it. Then Walter trotted away in one direction, Katie in the other.

Although Katie loved Walter the horse, she wasn't quite so crazy about dogs, especially little ones, who particularly irritated her. Heaven help a Boston terrier, Chihuahua, toy poodle, or Lhasa apso who got in her way. Ordinarily sweet little Katie would lash out at them, and bare her teeth, bark or snarl, sometimes even lunge at them, while I pulled back on the leash, scolding her.

"Stop it! Watch your manners. Bad girl. No!"

She'd look away from me with little remorse, tail wagging, having proven her dominance.

But she had much greater regard for more imposing dogs like golden retrievers, Great Danes, German shepherds, and Labs. These mighty canines were worthy of her respect and congenial sniffing, and none of them intimidated her. The bigger the dog, the more she liked it.

Katie was absolutely fearless strutting up to an eighty-pounder, almost three times her weight, poking her nose into theirs, licking them or whacking them playfully in the face with her paw.

One day, in our lobby, when a neighbor's Great Dane named Barney flattened her to the ground with his humongous paw, she laughed it off, rolling on her back before standing up again and licking him on the nose. Then, she marched into the elevator without a second glance, dismissing the brute.

Because Katie had no canine brother or sister or regular playmates, her true passion was people, though, again, it depended on their size—and age.

She vehemently disliked young kids and avoided them at all costs because of their unpredictability. If they even tried to pet her, she'd run away, casting an angry look. And the only time I ever heard her growl or even bark was when they persisted, attempting to pull on her ears or yank her tail. Then she'd let out a high-pitched howl. *"Ouch, Dad!"* she seemed to say. *"They hurt me—and I'm scared. Can't those kids leave me alone?"* She'd be screeching as she alternately lunged forward or hid behind me.

But when she was socializing with adults, whether in my living room, in the lobby, or outside on the Esplanade, she was an expert mingler. Katie not only recognized the colorful cast of human characters in her life, but reacted to each of them differently.

For example, she learned that Arthur's legs bothered him, so she never jumped up on him, understanding that her rightful place was on his gray velour chair and ottoman, her head balanced on his foot as he read the newspaper.

Katie also knew that she was never to jump up on our frail, across-the-hall neighbor Freda, a retired family-court judge who walked with braces due to childhood polio.

"Hello Katie, how are you today?" she'd inquire rather formally, greeting us as we both approached our front doors. Katie sat respectfully in front of the judge and simply offered a paw.

"She has excellent manners," laughed Freda, "much better than some who came before my bench!"

In truth, Katie adored just about *anybody* over the age of seventy—the older the better. I believe it was because she felt safe with them. In addition to Pearl, Arthur, and Freda, she gravitated to her regular "pack," a group of elderly residents all in their seventies, eighties, and nineties.

In the spring, summer, and fall months, each night after dinner, Pearl and Arthur would set out for the Esplanade to watch the sunset while I usually headed out for a bike ride, looping around the path along the Hudson River to enjoy the startling view. The brilliant red-and-orange sunlight glowed as it descended against the sky, lighting up the water and the Statue of Liberty.

"Hurry, I don't want to miss it," Arthur would exclaim, briskly tying the laces of his sneakers as Katie interfered, biting on them.

"Stop it, girlie, we've got to *go!*" And Katie would spring to the door, now anxious to be hitched up to her leash for the evening ritual.

Pearl and Arthur would then head west toward their favorite bench facing the marina, Katie trailing behind them as she scouted for regulars. There was the vivacious, wickedly clever Georgie, who talked in a gravelly smoker's voice; the hard-of-hearing, rather stiff and proper millionairess, Sally; the tall, athletic retired headmistress of a private girls' academy, Ruth, who swam laps each morning in our pool; the petite college professor in towering high heels, Sylvia, who always spoke in a whisper; the corpulent and boisterous retired businessman Brody; the shy, slim Chanel-attired Gloria, always floating in a mist of Tiffany perfume; and the eldest, Georgia, ninety, in a wheelchair, accompanied by her delightful and devoted daughter, Anita.

Spotting the wheelchair from quite a distance, Katie would spring out of Pearl's arms, leap off the bench, and run over to greet Georgia. She'd then protectively lead her over to Pearl and the rest of the group.

Having successfully herded her entire gang together, Katie sat contentedly as everyone gazed out at the sailboats and private yachts floating on the Hudson. Katie was typically balanced on Pearl's lap, blissfully taking it all in as she snacked on a banana.

One summer night as Katie sat with her regulars, I noticed her leaning her head dreamily against Georgia's arm, her big brown eyes batting away. What a flirt.

"She's such a lover," Georgia marveled, never suspecting Katie's fire and passion, which erupted weekly when it came to greeting my longtime housekeeper Ramon.

As you might remember from earlier, Ramon was originally terrified of Katie, and threatened to quit when I got her, but not anymore.

"Hiya Katie girl, what's up?" he'd now ask playfully. Katie got breathless with excitement whenever she saw him. My dog was crazier about Ramon than *anybody* else. Nobody, including me, got a more ecstatic greeting than him.

On Tuesdays, when the doorman buzzed to tell me that Ramon was on his way up, I'd open the door, clap my hands, and let Katie loose as I made a sound similar to a cowboy herding horses.

She could just smell him coming—and galloped down the hallway in a frenzy as he came off the elevator, then jumping up on him and wildly running in circles as she beckoned him toward my door with her head.

Once inside, she'd throw herself down on the living room carpet, and like an acrobat, roll over and over, begging him to stroke her tummy. Amazingly, he started doing it.

"Okay, Okay, Okay...Yes, yes, yes girlie...show it to me!" he'd tease, giving her vigorous belly rubs. "You like it?" She was in ecstasy and I'd tease Ramon that he got her more excited than food.

And after that, as Ramon worked, Katie followed him around for the entire four hours. When he was folding laundry, she laid her head on the warm towels, angelically looking up at him; when he was in the bathtub scrubbing down the tiles, she was just outside it, lounging on the floor, keeping a watchful eye; and when he was vacuuming, she stood just behind him, fascinated by the electric cord and often tripping over it.

"Get OUT of my way, Katie!" he'd tell her. But she never did. Their friendship would last Katie's entire lifetime.

In contrast to the ecstasy she felt at seeing Ramon, Katie was totally uninterested in her two regular dog walkers—a sweet Chinese woman named Ann, who adored my dog, and her nephew, Ken, the business brains behind their Battery Park dog-walking operation. The thought of leaving Pearl's cozy nest for a mandatory walk with either of them was unappealing to Katie.

"Kay-teeeee," Ann would sing in high-pitched singsong, waltzing into Pearl's apartment to retrieve her charge. She'd plant a big kiss on Pearl's cheek, often bringing her apples or oranges as treats.

"Kay-teeeee," Ann continued. But Katie played deaf, hiding under Pearl's twin bed, burrowing toward the center of it, knowing she was too far to reach. Ann would laugh and have to either bribe Katie out with a cookie or literally drag her out by her front paws. Katie always resisted, her sharp nails digging into the tan carpet, her head down.

At other times, Katie would attempt to camouflage herself on the lowest shelf of a mahogany bookcase where Pearl had placed a soft towel. She'd lean into that shelf like a magician trying to blend into the scenery, hiding from view, determined to evade capture. But ultimately, tail down, she'd reluctantly trail out of the apartment for a walk.

On rainy days, Ann hitched Katie into her blue-and-white slicker, the two sides of the coat connecting with Velcro. Katie gingerly put her paws into the four holes and off they went. Once back inside, Pearl would be waiting at the door with a towel, ready to dry Katie off from the indignity of being soaked to the bone. She'd rub-a-dub-dub away at Katie's wet head, ears, and body, and then wrap her in a big fluffy towel as if Katie were at a spa, with only her face poking out. Finally dry, Katie would vigorously shake herself and then leap onto Pearl's soft bed for some relaxing television, not to be budged until dinner.

Some nights, Katie would wrest herself from Pearl's side, returning to my apartment ahead of schedule, discerning and curious to judge any new friends. Jealousy was clearly a prime factor.

If she liked the person—the vibe or smell they gave off—she'd crawl into their lap and snuggle close, seducing them with her charms. But if she didn't, she'd hide and refuse to accept even a pat on the back.

Or worse. On one occasion, a friend who was a pastry chef was whipping up a chocolate pot de crème in my kitchen. Katie seemed especially receptive, feigning interest in exchange for some whipped cream. But later that night, after the snack, she whacked her paw against his face, knocking his eyeglasses to the floor, then sat down on them, refusing to budge.

"Naughty! No! Bad dog!" I yelled. She slinked away, tail down, though she had a sly look on her face, her tongue hanging out of her mouth, a sure sign that she had no regrets.

The ultimate insult, of course, was the rare occasion when she'd take one look at a prospective competitor for my affection and relieve herself.

Such were her strong opinions.

CHAPTER NINE

A Real Pearl

Katie idolized her mom down the hall and followed Pearl around incessantly, while she also continued her busybody walks at sunset—herding together the pack of seniors who had adopted her as their prized mascot.

But outside of Manhattan, my dog's favorite person was my grandmother, Essie. Each Thanksgiving when we went home to Buffalo, Nana fussed over Katie, and, later, actively kept tabs on her adventures in New York via the phone.

I can still see Nana and Katie sitting together on the orange velvet couch in my mom's living room—Nana combing out Katie's ears as my dog snoozed in her lap, oblivious to being primped while deliciously comforted by my grandmother's presence.

Very sadly, my Nana died of bone cancer in 1990 at age ninety-one, her passing leaving a great hole in our family—and in my heart.

Katie went to Nana's funeral, sitting obediently at the graveside, her ears blowing in the brisk November wind. Later that day, she climbed into my mom's lap to comfort her, licking her face.

"I'll never forget when Katie crawled up on top of me," my mom later reflected, "put her head right under my chin, and laid her paw on my chest, hugging me all night long. She never let go."

Especially after Nana's death, slowly, imperceptibly, Pearl became even more important to me, my all-in-one confidante, best neighborhood friend, surrogate grandmother, and comrade-in-arms.

Being able to see her daily was a real luxury, a happy treat for me and Katie. There was Pearl at the door, standing with ramrod posture, a look of wry expectation on her face—a blend of affection, amusement, and genuine interest.

Like the captain of a ship at the wheel, she was usually stationed at her dining table, peeling apples, shucking corn, or cutting up zucchini. I joined her there and we shot the breeze on pretty much everything—from my celebrity interviews to dating, from world headlines to healthy eating, though Katie was always topic number one.

We had nicknamed Katie "the child," jokingly pronounced "chaaa-aellll-d," and when I'd walk in, I'd typically ask: "How's my sweet little chaaa-aellll-d doin' today?"

"Your *child* stole my best napkin out of the linen closet—the one my mother embroidered—and turned it into this!" Pearl announced dramatically, holding up the shredded linen.

"Bad girl!" I lectured Katie, showing her the decimated napkin as she sniffed it with disinterest, having had her way with it.

"What are you going to do to make it up to me?" Pearl asked. Katie licked her hand in penance, the fastest way back into Pearl's good graces. All was quickly forgiven as Pearl hugged her girl tightly.

"Girlie," Pearl would ask, "you want an *apple*?"

Katie knew that word like her own name, and would leap on the dining room chair and wait for Pearl to pop one little chunk of a red delicious after another into her mouth.

"What about a *cookie*?" Katie trotted over to the cookie jar, hitting it with her paw.

"My girl want to *dance*?" Katie threw up her front paws at Pearl, prancing on her back legs as Pearl sang, "*I wanna be in pictures...I wanna be a star.*"

I quickly discovered the many facets of our Pearl.

She could be extremely girlish at times, and feisty at others.

"She was a serious, plain woman, not a game player," my mom once observed, "and she sometimes had a gruff look on her face. You had to get to know her. She was what she was— and made no bones about it."

But just underneath her no-nonsense exterior was a layer of kindness and pathos that reflected itself in her complete interest in others. Never one to reveal much about her emotions, she much preferred putting the focus on her guests during visits to her apartment.

"She was a very good listener," my mom noted. "But when she wanted you to leave—you knew it!"

For most people, this was true, but the relationship as it developed between us was so comfortable that I never felt as if I was imposing on her time, and vice versa.

One day, when Pearl and Arthur came by to show off their outfits and pose for pictures before they left for an afternoon wedding, she was all giggles. "I have a handsome date, don't I? And I'm not bad myself," Pearl winked, outfitted in a pale green silk suit, simple gold jewelry, and patent leather shoes with bows.

But when I gave Pearl some advice too forwardly about

having her windows professionally cleaned (something they desperately needed), she snapped, "Mind your own business! I like the spots." Case closed. She wasn't about to pay for that luxury.

As I knew, Pearl was conservative about money, with coupons frequently in hand, yet immensely generous, often taking clothes to the homeless or making dinner for friends at loose ends. And underlying her sometimes prickly demeanor and sarcastic wit were compassion for people's frailties and a cautious realism born of the Great Depression.

"You spend too much money!" she lectured me, over and over again. "Katie doesn't need five winter coats...take that one back."

Yes, Ma'am.

Soon enough, our long dining room table chats became habit-forming and were often accompanied by something good to eat. On the way home from work, stopping in nearby Greenwich Village, I'd pick up Pearl and Arthur's favorite Italian pastries from Veniero's or Rocco's, or I'd get glazed cookies from Jon Vie, or crispy Italian bread from Zito's, any of it cause for celebration.

During this period, out of nowhere, I came up with the nickname "Pa-Re-El," affectionately calling out Pearl's name in a stretched-out cattle call, that started low, went high on "Re," and ended lower on the syllable "El." I'd get home with the goodies and knock on her door, letting out that unmistakable "Pa-Re-El."

She'd laugh good-naturedly as she beckoned me toward the dining table, drawn by the mystery of the white bakery box in my hands.

Arthur would emerge from the bedroom in a rush, clap his hands, and Katie would fly out from the bed as if she'd been shot from a cannon. She'd jump in one leap onto the dining chair at the prospect of a cannoli or sliver of ricotta cheesecake.

Over numerous visits and dozens of Italian pastries, I learned more and more about Pearl and Arthur's history and was intrigued by it, piecing together snippets of information as the calories mounted.

⌗

Born in New York City in 1912, Pearl and her older sister, Stella ("the pretty one," she laughed), were raised in a middle-class Jewish family in the Kingsbridge section of the West Bronx. The young Pearl doted on her little fox terrier.

Pearl's mother, Ray, was a perfectionist, an excellent cook and astute homemaker, while her father, Isadore, nicknamed "Doc," very distinguished in wire-rim glasses, was a rep for a women's clothing manufacturer, selling piece goods.

Although the vivacious Pearl was a very bright girl with natural wit, she had little interest in her studies, but much interest in boys.

"I was supposed to marry a doctor—my parents had him all picked out for me—talk about handsome!" she laughed, remembering her beau with relish.

"Yeah, maybe he was handsome—big deal—but I came along," interjected Arthur.

"Yes, at Christmas 1934, I was working part-time at the perfume counter in Macy's," Pearl explained, "and Arthur came by looking for a gift for his mother. *I* was the gift! And he wasn't bad looking either."

"I was irresistible," mugged Arthur, explaining that his family worked as house painters, "and that doctor was history."

The young couple hit it off immediately and discovered that they coincidentally lived just a few doors down from one another on Aqueduct Avenue. It was love at first sight.

In 1935, though her parents thought she was too young, the twenty-three-year-old Pearl forged ahead and married "the boy next door."

Despite the fast repartee and easy affection between Pearl and Arthur during our visits, I sensed a mild sadness hanging in the air, a sense of loss or regret. I couldn't quite put my finger on it until a few years after I met them, when I finally understood the missing link.

As it turned out, early in their marriage, Pearl became pregnant—and the couple was ecstatic. But their happiness was short-lived.

Three months into her pregnancy, an ovarian tumor was discovered. A stricken Pearl was told that if it wasn't promptly removed, it could threaten her life. She wound up having the surgery, which included a hysterectomy, and, of course, she lost the baby.

This was the tragedy that Pearl never discussed.

Although Pearl and Arthur had initially gotten a little Bronx apartment of their own after getting married, Pearl was so depressed after the surgery that she and Arthur wound up moving back home to live with her parents, Doc and Ray.

Recovering slowly in the nurturing environment of home, Pearl's spirits revived and, a few years later, Arthur was drafted into the Navy.

Although he rarely talked about his experiences during World War II, Arthur repeatedly reminisced about his favorite on-ship friend, a pet monkey. One day, he dug into a shoebox of ancient photos and pulled out a picture of himself as a bare-chested young sailor, holding up his precocious primate. "That monkey had more sense than some of my mates," he laughed.

"And sometimes more than you," ribbed Pearl.

After the war, Pearl worked as a secretary, typing up notes

for a writer—"I earned $12 a week and gave my mother $5"—while Arthur was a salesman of wholesale women's apparel. All the while, they continued living with Pearl's parents. One year drifted into the next, and decades slipped by, and Pearl and Arthur wound up living with Pearl's parents for nearly their entire married life!

In fact, they remained in the Bronx until they themselves were in their seventies, caring for Ray and Doc until their deaths, then staying on to care for Arthur's mother until *her* death. Their only respite from family duty was the small country home in Dutchess County that they enjoyed on weekends.

So amazingly, Pearl and Arthur almost never lived alone as a couple until they moved to Battery Park City in 1983.

At last, they were on their own, though a profound vacuum was left behind, the proximity of family gone.

And by the time I met them, even their beloved cocker spaniel Brandy had passed away.

As a result, Pearl and Arthur were wide open to a new chapter in their lives—and adopted Katie and me as their brand-new family.

⌗

At first prim about her personal business, Pearl gradually confided more of her intimate feelings about many things, as we became closer and closer.

She was disappointed, for example, in some of her family members with whom she'd cut off relations, though she adored her grand-niece, Susan, who lived in London, and her grand-nephew, James, in Boston. Like all good aunts, she bragged about their accomplishments, showing me their cards and letters, though she regretted they only visited about once or twice a year.

Private as she was, she would never have told them how much she worried about her finances ("we're living on a strict budget") and what serious concerns she had about Arthur's health (he often had colds, bronchial infections, and intense pain due to arthritis).

"Arthur was always so strong—and he used to take me dancing in Atlantic City," she smiled, looking over at her prized photo, taken on her honeymoon there. In it, Pearl was wearing a fur-trimmed coat and looked very chic, while Arthur was quite debonair in a blue blazer and white slacks.

"But now he spends so much of his time in bed," she frowned, though she was determined to keep him strong by buying his favorite foods and going to the farmers' market for fruits and vegetables.

I marveled at Pearl's sheer energy. Nearly eighty, she was sturdily built and rarely sick, and did all her own shopping, cooking, and cleaning, while also taking superb care of Arthur (and, of course, Katie).

"I got my little girlie some dog vitamins today," she told Katie one day, popping a chewable pill into my dog's mouth before she could resist, then following it with a Milk-Bone chaser. "Now go over by the window and get some sun," she ordered. And off Katie went, stretching out on her back for a snooze.

Pearl also took excellent care of me—treating me as the grandson she never had. Like my own grandmother had, she kindly picked up my favorite rye bread with black seeds, spoiled me with Nova Scotia salmon and cream cheese, and did neighborly things like getting the mail or taking packages in when I was out of town.

And although she wasn't very physically demonstrative, I could sense her love and affection just by the way she looked at me or touched my shoulder or arm.

She was a great date and we sometimes went to movies

together (leaving Arthur at home reading, as he preferred it), to Broadway shows, out for dinner or shopping, or on long walks along the Esplanade with Katie.

Pa-Re-El and I now shared a unique closeness. But "the child's" daily antics, needs, and moods remained the centrifugal force that bonded us.

❦

In 1992, Katie turned four, celebrating it with a carrot cake. The cream cheese frosting covered her mouth as she munched happily away on it, pulling each piece off a fork held by Pearl.

By this point, I noticed an almost mystical bond between Katie and Pearl, notwithstanding Katie's close relationship to Arthur as well.

My dog simply worshipped Pearl. She lay on her kitchen floor when she cooked, napped on the living room couch when she cleaned, and lounged on her bed as they both watched TV—typically the Food Channel.

One day when Pearl was watching the *Oprah Winfrey Show*, Katie irritated her by pressing her paw down on the remote control (something she saw Pearl do all the time) and accidentally changing channels.

"No!" snapped Pearl, taking the remote away from Katie and switching it back to ABC.

But Katie persisted, grabbing it back again, and slapping down her paw on the buttons. It seemed that she understood the connection between her action and the changing of pictures and sounds. And I could tell by her mesmerized expression that she was enjoying the mischievous game.

"No!" Pearl repeated, hiding the remote under her pillow and leaning against it as Katie attempted to flush it out again.

"She's Queen Katie," Pearl told me later that day, "but smart as a whip."

She was also, of course, hungry all the time. Katie especially irritated Pearl when she used the remote control as a dog bone, biting into it with gusto. "That girl knows what she wants and she's spoiled rotten." I knew that well, as I was the one who had spoiled her.

Whatever that dog wanted, she got.

Sometimes when Pearl was on the phone, Katie would sit up on the bed rather regally and slap Pearl on the arm with her paw, "telling" her to get off the line and pay some attention to her.

"Come on, Pa-Re-El," she seemed to say, *"Let's play!"*

At other times, she'd seduce Pearl into a nap by stretching out on her back, placing her head on Pearl's pillow, and pulling Pearl over in her direction.

More than once, I'd find them snoozing blissfully together, the Food Channel lulling them both to sleep. On nights like those, I didn't dare wake them, so Katie got a sleepover, while Arthur got a surprise.

CHAPTER TEN

Everything That Goes Up . . .

The year 1992 was a wonderful one for me.

On May 15, as I blew the candles out on my birthday cake at an outdoor fortieth birthday party set up overlooking the Hudson River, everything in my world seemed just about perfect.

The weather that night was sublime, warm and breezy, with sailboats drifting by as we picnicked on the shore.

Katie was in great spirits, spunkier than ever, trotting around the guests outfitted with a pink birthday hat that was perched crookedly on her head.

Pearl and Arthur had their "girl" on a red leash as they talked animatedly with my family, friends, and colleagues from work.

And to top it all off, I had completed a new book that would be published in the fall. It was titled *Turning Point: Pivotal Moments in the Lives of America's Celebrities*, a compilation of 120 interviews featuring celebrities who had talked to me about how they'd overcome crises in their lives, based upon the column I was writing in the *New York Daily News*.

Here were conversations with everyone from Mary Tyler

Moore, Carol Burnett, Dolly Parton, and Paul Newman to Calvin Klein, Malcolm Forbes, Walter Cronkite, and Joan Kennedy.

I dedicated the book to you-know-who. Her picture graced the title page with this inscription: "To my baby, Katie, the sweetest turning point I've known—a daily reminder of innocence, loyalty, and love."

Pearl and Arthur were my full-time "grandparents," proud, doting, and excited about the book and also eager to read my magazine stories. The lineup that year would include Elizabeth Taylor ("Behind the Mask: AIDS & the Celebrity Crusade"), Marla Maples ("The Marla 'Follies'"), Kathie Lee Gifford ("Believe It!"), Michael Jackson ("Soul Survivor"), Al Pacino ("Happy at Last?"), and Cher ("Total Cher").

Each time I got an advance copy of one of these stories, I took it right home for a ritual "show and tell," which always took place around Pearl's trusty dining table.

One day, I remember Arthur opening up the pages to an interview with Sylvester Stallone, while Katie pushed around him, poking her nose into the magazine pages and scratching them with her paws, vying for attention.

"Calm down, girlie, and eat your bone," he ordered, gently pushing her away as he became engrossed in the story.

Beyond being my most avid reader, Arthur was a trusted friend and advised me on anything and everything—house repairs, choice of suits, financial investments, medical care for Katie, and strategies for handling my boss. I found the soothing sound of his raspy baritone voice calming, and he always put things into perspective for me as nobody else could.

And Pearl was no less helpful, handing out advice and recipes, conveying the latest health tip she'd heard on the radio, reminding me about neighborhood events, and giving me the thumbs-up or thumbs-down on a prospective date or friend.

We were a family.

I couldn't have loved my own grandparents any more than I did Pearl and Arthur. We seemed to fulfill within one another a deep need for connection—and it didn't hurt that we were so accessible to one another, separated by just forty-five feet.

By fall of that year, I was promoting *Turning Point*, first on the *Oprah Winfrey Show*, which devoted an entire show to the book, featuring four of my interview subjects, each one of them talking about challenging moments in their lives. There was Marla Maples (on Donald Trump), Rod Steiger (on depression), Angie Dickinson (on her sister's diagnosis of Alzheimer's disease), and Annette Funicello (on her battling multiple sclerosis).

Oprah, as always, was astutely sensitive as she navigated through people's darkest moments, finding the uplifting lesson in each of them.

And then, the lightest, most entertaining moment of the show came when Oprah asked me about Leona Helmsley's "turning point,"—going off to jail.

"What did she tell you?" Oprah asked curiously.

I offered just one sentence—"LET ME OUT!"—which brought us to the commercial break with good-natured, uproarious laughter.

After this broadcast, both Sally Jessy Raphael and Geraldo Rivera followed with shows of their own on the book, though the most lighthearted approach to the turning point theme was on Joan Rivers's show, as few could equal her dry wit and appetite for mischief.

Joan had been my first celebrity interview back in 1983,

and over the years, I'd interviewed her many times, most emotionally after her husband, Edgar, had committed suicide.

I was always struck that such a brilliantly funny woman was, off-stage, so serious and thoughtful, though onstage that day we reveled in some mildly risqué celebrity hounding.

The most entertaining part of the interview was when she asked about Joan Collins's past marriages and predilection for younger men. I told her, "Joan says the sex is better with younger men…much better…and no back pain!" The audience started laughing while the faux taken-aback expression on Joan's face made the moment even funnier.

The book tour ended on a high note with a mid-December appearance on *Larry King*. The studio was freezing, as I remember, but Larry struck me as incredibly warm and down to earth, welcoming a noncelebrity like me as if I were one.

For the book, Larry had discussed his recovery from a 1987 heart attack, "If you want to know the moment, the turning point, it was opening my eyes after the surgery. 'Mr. King, you did terrific!' is what the nurse said. From that moment on, my life changed. After that," he told me, "I threw my cigarettes in the Potomac," along with the Oreo cookies and pizza, determined to change his habits. "Now I'm on the treadmill every day and went from 190 pounds to 160."

"Happy at last?" I asked him.

"I'm a nine on the scale—still that little Jewish kid from Brooklyn wanting approval from the outside. There's no ten. Maybe next year."

As for me, on a scale of one to ten, I certainly felt as if 1992 had been a ten. After the show that night, sitting in a Washington, DC, hotel suite, I counted my blessings.

And a week later, on New Year's Eve, Arthur, Pearl and I

ushered in the New Year with Champagne. Katie wore a New Year's hat and had a few sips before snoozing her way into 1993 — just slightly tipsy.

Then everything crashed — and it happened so fast.

One minute I was answering questions from Larry King's viewers about how people overcome crises; and the next, I was having a crisis of my own.

Just two weeks after Larry's show, in January 1993, my professional world as I knew it imploded — everything I had built up was quickly taken away.

The newspaper where I worked, the financially beleaguered *Daily News*, had been sold by the Tribune Company to the new owner, Mort Zuckerman, and 180 employees were fired — including me. I suddenly had no job and no income. Gone were the syndicated column, the Sunday magazine cover stories, the TV shows, the access to celebrities — and along with them, my position in the world.

Now I was on the unemployment line. God does have an excellent sense of humor. Looking back, I can now see that my ego had become supersized — inflated with all those stars who made me feel more important than I was. Clearly, I was not indispensable. And although I tried to get another job, the market was flooded with deposed *Daily News* troops, and it just wasn't happening.

By the late winter of 1993, I was truly demoralized. I had gone from hero to zero in a matter of weeks. And despite my past productivity, I felt like a complete failure.

Superdisciplined, I was used to being out of my apartment by 7:30 a.m. and gone until 9:00 p.m. But now I was home all day, disoriented by this turnaround. It's easy to feel satisfied when things are going your way, but feeling good under adverse circumstances takes a lot more strength than I had. That's when you really need your friends, family—and your dog.

Although I was off-kilter, Katie insisted on keeping to her routine—racing down the hallway right after breakfast to Pearl's just as before, though I did manage to snatch her back in the afternoons, going out for long walks with her and giving her more of my attention than she was accustomed to.

As for Pearl and Arthur, they were, as always, nonjudgmental and encouraging. "Something will turn around for you," said Arthur. Most therapeutic were our dinners together when we talked about Katie and the neighborhood rather than focusing on "the problem."

Then, one March day, with a snowstorm blasting Battery Park City, I was outside walking up a steep hill, feeling rather morose, when my back snapped, the muscles locking in spasm. I had always had back pain, which tended to worsen with excessive sitting, bending, or stress, but this had rarely happened. I could barely move and hobbled home bent at a ninety-degree angle.

Over the next weeks, Pearl mobilized into action, more helpful than ever. My injury seemed to energize her. (That made one of us.) She took Katie outside for walks and ministered to all the dog caretaking—feeding her, playing with her, brushing out her coat. She also helped me change the sheets on the bed, picked up medicine at the drugstore, went food shopping, and collected the mail.

And most nights she'd come by with an entire dinner in hand: hot soup, a salad, grilled salmon, spaghetti, tuna casserole, or breaded chicken cutlets, followed by a tart or cake.

Katie licked her chops, stealing as much of the food as possible while cheering me up as I sat there against pillows with either an ice pack or heating pad under me.

"The child now moves a lot better than you do!" joked Pa-Re-El, marveling at Katie's gymnastics as she jumped on the bed, dragging a sock over to me for a game of tug-of-war.

Katie, Pearl, and Arthur did more to boost my spirits than any job could have. I appreciated them now, more than ever, and having them close to me was incredibly comforting.

Over the next few months, after visits to an orthopedic surgeon, a chiropractor, pain specialists, and a physical therapist, I learned that I would have to drastically change my lifestyle—no more sitting for long periods writing, no bending, no running, limited exercise, and no more *working*.

Now I was really depressed. How did I go so quickly from being "able" to "disabled"? Sure, I could walk and do the basics, but my world, as I had known it, was drastically changed—and all in three months.

I needed help (and not just the physical kind). And I found it, in early January, at a Community Center located on West 13th Street in Greenwich Village. This was a fantastic place offering social events, support groups, twelve-step meetings, and a wide array of health, youth, and family services—a total of 14,000 activities per year.

I started attending support groups almost daily, which immeasurably helped jolt me from depression and connected me to my peers. People talked about everything here—from their finances and job challenges to the ups and downs of relationships, family issues, physical health, and addiction matters as well.

One freezing day in February, when I brought Katie along with me into the dog-friendly Community Center, we were just hanging out in the main reception area on the ground floor, enjoying the parade of people going in and out.

Amid all the adults, I noticed a tiny little boy racing around the room, making wide loops, whooping it up, giggling uproariously as he circled us. He was the cutest kid imaginable, with brownish-golden bangs that fell into those beguiling brown eyes, his plump little face lit up with a sparkling smile.

Outfitted in a Mickey Mouse T-shirt, blue corduroy pants, and black-and-white sneakers (with blinking red lights that illuminated when he ran), he reminded me of Dennis the Menace — a boy filled with high spirits and mischievous plans.

Katie, who was ordinarily frightened of kids and loud noises (and averse to having her space invaded), jumped out of my arms and stood still as a statue, legs spread in combat position, warily watching this boisterous boy.

"Don't be afraid, he won't hurt you," I soothed her, giving her a pat on the butt and nudging her forward, encouraging her to play.

"*But Dad*," she seemed to say, "*I'm not so sure. That kid looks dangerous . . . but running looks like fun. I do like to race!*"

"Then go ahead," I told her, letting her off the leash.

In a flash, Katie threw caution to the wind and took off, skipping after the exuberant boy. When she caught up to him, she started off hesitantly, sniffing his leg, but she was soon chasing him.

The boy became even more energized, running faster, delighted to have a companion. They whirled together, around and around the room, disturbing everyone in their wake. Katie's tail stood up in delight. The little kid let out a mock scream, as if he was threatened by her pursuit, though I could tell he knew he wasn't in any danger.

This had *never* happened before. Katie had always disliked kids and avoided them — but now she was elated. She actually bounced up against the boy to embrace him, offering her paw to "shake," a big grin on her face, her tongue hanging out, breathless with happiness.

"Hi girl!" the boy smiled, stopping for just a minute to pet her, then screaming, "Now let's GO!" And off they went again, fast new friends, the boy dodging people drinking their coffee as he led the way around the perimeter of the room.

"But who *is* that little dude?" I asked, talking half out loud to myself, wondering why he was left unattended.

"His name is Ryan—and I'm his father John!" laughed a blond-haired, affable-looking guy in his late thirties, coming up behind me.

I'd seen John in the support group before, and he was a very approachable person—warm, talkative, and relaxed. He wore glasses and had blue eyes and an easygoing smile.

Midwestern in appearance, he was dressed in a plaid flannel shirt, corduroy pants, and a bulky ski parka, both rugged and slightly bookish looking. Here was a real person with solid values, someone with no pretense or artifice. He put me right at ease.

I had heard him describe the challenges, and rewards, of raising a son as a single gay dad, and I knew that he was active as one of only three men in the Community Center's single parents' group—part of the "Center Kids" program. One thing that came across loud and clear was his utter devotion to his son.

"Ryan's two-and-a-half and he loves dogs," John told me, pulling up a chair. "In fact, as you can see, he never leaves home without one." And there, tucked under the boy's arm was a raggedy stuffed animal, a golden retriever.

"That's Puppy!" John told me, "though it looks like Ryan has found a new puppy."

"I'm a single parent too, kind of," I joked. "That's

Katie—and she never does this. In fact, she *hates* kids—but not today."

As John and I chatted, I discovered that we had much in common. After graduating from Stanford in computer science, he had gotten a master's degree in journalism from Northwestern University and now worked at the *New York Times*. I told him about my fall from grace at the *Daily News* and he commiserated, though our focus was mostly on our "kids," one human, one canine.

"Ryan," John explained, "has aunts and uncles and cousins, but none of them close by."

I learned that John was one of five, raised in Chicago, and that, sadly, at age nine, he had lost his mother to cancer, while his father had later died when John was in college. It wasn't easy growing up without a mother, and now, with his siblings living out West, John wanted to carve out a family of his own.

Perhaps, I thought, he was filling in a space in a heart that had weathered much loss. Or maybe, as I later understood, he just loved kids and wanted to raise one.

John and Ryan lived in nearby Montclair, New Jersey. Having recently broken up with a long-term partner, John was determined to move into New York City to start a new life.

"The commute," he explained, "is becoming unmanageable. Every morning, I take Ryan to day care, get on a bus, come into Manhattan to work, then back to day care and home again. I've *got* to find an apartment in Manhattan."

"You should definitely look in Battery Park City," I told him. "I love it there," joking that our complex's 300 dogs would keep Ryan quite busy.

"I never even thought of it," he said.

"Well, it's an incredible neighborhood—right on the water

with a marina, and boats, and a view of the Statue—and it's filled with families, hundreds of kids, and a great elementary school."

The next day, I brought John downtown to show him around, and our rental office put him on a waiting list for a two-bedroom apartment. "It will be at least six months," he was told, which left John worried as he had to move by May.

But then, in April, the agent called, "We've got *one* two-bedroom available, so you'd better come look at it now. It will be gone by the end of the day."

When John got downtown, I was puzzled when the agent brought him up to *my* floor.

"Where are we headed?" I asked.

"We're here!" the agent laughed, taking us down the hallway to apartment 3P.

I couldn't believe that the *only* apartment available in our entire six-building complex of over 1,700 units was an apartment right down the hall from me.

"What were the chances of this happening?" I asked John.

"It must be about one in a million," he laughed, delighted by the coincidence.

John took apartment 3P the next day.

"Was that fate?" I later asked him.

"Oh, absolutely. It was a higher power intervening. It would never have been the same if I'd been living on a different floor or in a different building."

❦

My reversal of fortune (losing my job and getting sick) forced me to slow down, to rest and reflect. And with the time to do this, my life was beginning to turn in an unexpectedly positive direction, with new people and activities in it. This change—which also allowed me to spend more time with Katie—was about to present surprises and adventures that I never could have imagined.

As that spring ended, I continued attending support group meetings with John at the Community Center. Part of my "therapy" included participating in a theatrical production, a spoof of *The Wizard of Oz*.

I played the Scarecrow and Katie was cast as Toto. The old adage about never taking the stage with a baby or an animal proved true. Katie, a born entertainer, stole the show. She strutted around, tail wagging, ran down the yellow brick road after being seduced by a piece of chicken, and whirled in circles as she attempted to bite the Wicked Witch, growling on cue.

At the curtain call, with the applause pouring over her, Katie took her "bow" the wrong way, rolling on her back and spreading her legs ("No, Katie, sit!").

Quickly correcting herself, she then scanned the audience, happily spotting Ryan, and raised her paw in thanks before running offstage for a cookie.

CHAPTER ELEVEN

Canine Cop

Three Apartments Become One

L inden trees were in full bloom in June 1993 when John and Ryan moved in. Our tree-lined Esplanade, abundant with beds of roses and hydrangeas, was filled with joggers and bikers, while the Hudson River was brimming with activity of every kind.

"Daddy, look at the *boats*!" hollered a wildly excited Ryan, transfixed at their living room window by the procession of motorboats and cruise liners.

The three-year-old, who loved miniature cars and anything on wheels, was almost bouncing off the walls that day, overwhelmed by the sights and sounds of his new neighborhood.

There wasn't too much furniture to unload, as John owned just the basics, though there was no shortage of toys.

"No, Katie!" I shouted, grabbing out of her mouth a metal toy soldier that she was about to choke on. She then switched gears, snooping into each carton of playthings. She pulled out rubber ducks Ryan used in the tub and stuffed animals, shaking them around in her mouth, while Ryan kicked his soccer ball off the living room wall.

"Stop that, Ryan!" ordered John, rolling his eyes at me, unfazed by the controlled chaos. "You play soccer out in the hall."

Katie was puzzled by the ball's size, though she soon caught on to pushing it forward with her nose or paws, and within minutes, the twosome were chasing it down the hallway.

Despite the stresses of moving, John was, as usual, calm and controlled, allowing Ryan his freedom while keeping a watchful eye over him.

As a single parent, John was both Mom and Dad to his young son. And I noticed how skillfully he combined the best of both the maternal and paternal. He was a masculine guy, a newspaper sports editor who loved soccer, football, and computers, but was also highly sensitive and expressive. He was gently nurturing to Ryan and physically affectionate to him in the way a mom might be. Ryan would often curl up in John's lap, his head resting on his shoulder, as John read to him.

"We're going to have a blessing of our new apartment here tonight," John told me, "and I'd like to invite you and Katie, Pearl, and Arthur to come over."

I'd never heard of doing something like this. But John, a member of St. John's in the Village Episcopal Church, explained that this was an ancient Jewish and Christian tradition observed centuries before, "one that has pretty much gone by the wayside in troubled times—and it's good to get it started again."

That evening, right at sunset, with the scent of the lindens drifting in from the water, there we were—Pearl, Arthur, John, Katie, and I—together with an Episcopal priest and a few friends close to John—all standing in a circle in John's living room, holding hands.

It was such a peaceful, heartwarming scene, different from

anything I'd experienced. "Being here," the priest explained, "is acknowledging the new members of our community—and blessing their new house, which is now a home. Make it a haven for all who will be here."

Pearl held onto Katie's red leash, and Katie was obedient, sitting quietly, sensing that something solemn was under way.

The priest then handed the Book of Common Prayer to Arthur, who was a devout Jew, though intrigued to be participating in the service. He loved ritual and prayer and actually recited a short Hebrew passage of blessing before switching back to the Episcopal reading, "Graciously receive our thanks for this place...and put far from those who dwell here every root of bitterness, the desire of vainglory, and the pride of life. Turn the hearts of the parents to the children and enkindle fervent charity among us all, that we may evermore be kindly affectioned one to another. Amen."

Although a few other passages followed, the words that really stuck with me that day were *affectioned one to another*— for that's exactly what happened—and quickly.

John and I became fast friends and we established an open-door policy that allowed all of us to freely visit up and down the hallway. As John later reflected, "I think you and I trusted each other—and you and Pearl were so close, which is why she decided to welcome us into the circle. Katie was the tie between you and Pearl and, of course, I loved dogs, and missed my dogs, so Katie became a welcome new member of our household too."

As for me, John's presence in our building was a healing balm, almost as if he were the brother I'd never had. We had dinner out, went to meetings, spent hours with "the kid" and Granny. He was also my on-the-spot tech whiz, as he could fix or install virtually anything—and did.

When I needed help with a computer crash, my Internet account, or a lesson on instant messaging, e-mail, or any other technical matter, there he was. One day, when all my financial files on Quicken disappeared, he offered to restore them, and did so successfully, though it took him hours at his office. This was typical of his generosity.

It was especially because I was out of work and having serious physical problems that his presence really lifted my spirits. It was such a luxury having a contemporary to talk to, right down the hall, comparable to dormitory living. Day or night, I could just walk the 120 feet from one apartment to another, ready for a chat. And Katie was always game to play with Ryan.

As John folded Ryan's laundry or assembled one of his many toys, we talked about anything and everything. We often shared observations about the people we knew at the Community Center, humorously roasting some of the quirkier characters we'd met. We also traded personal histories, exchanged war stories, and laughed riotously over the insanity of blind dates and the roller coaster of romance. Not one to give advice, John was an excellent listener who was expert at reflecting, philosophically, and talked about the importance of "letting go" and letting fate take its course. And of course, our main focus became Ryan and his blossoming connection to Katie, Pearl, Arthur, and me.

As I became closer to John, I could see that it wasn't easy being a single dad, acting as both mother and father—getting Ryan dressed, bathed, reading to him, and playing soccer while juggling a full-time job, plus shopping, cleaning, and cooking.

While he had previously shared child raising with his partner of thirteen years, the end of that relationship had left the entire burden on John. Sometimes he looked pretty exhausted by it all.

He needed help.

True, it was obvious that Ryan was well-adjusted and bliss-fully happy with "Daddy John," as he called him; but the fact remained that Ryan had no mother on the scene or grand-parents, while his uncles, aunts, and cousins were all in the Midwest.

That left *us*—and we were only too happy to pitch in.

As John later observed, "At the time we moved in, Pearl definitely became Ryan's surrogate grandmother. My mother and father were gone, there were no grandparents—so she was *it*!"

At first, though, Ryan experienced separation anxiety from his dad, as any child would.

One day, when John was away at work and I was babysit-ting, I took Ryan outside with me to the bank, Katie walking behind us. It broke my heart when Ryan suddenly started sob-bing on the street. "I miss my daddy!" he wailed. I got down on my knees, face to face, and Ryan crumbled in my arms as I wrapped him in a hug. Katie started licking the tears off Ryan's sweet face.

"Daddy loves you and so do I," I told him. "He'll be home very soon, I promise." And I then cheered him up by buying him an ice-cream cone. A wide smile lit up his face, then a frown as Katie stole as much of that strawberry scoop as she possibly could.

During my college years in Boston, I'd been a Big Brother to an eight-year-old named Kenny—and I loved doing it. I took Kenny to the park, museums, movies, and restaurants—and was very upset when I had to leave him, moving to Baltimore for graduate school. Kenny wrote me a good-bye note, saying, "Please don't ever forget me." And I never did.

And now, eighteen years later, another child had entered

my life, giving me another opportunity to offer what I could as a mentor and part-time babysitter.

At times when John was away, I filled up my bathtub with bubbles and Ryan climbed in with his rubber animals and boats. Katie watched from the sidelines as he blew bubbles at her. She hated having water splashed on her, and Ryan knew it, so he teased her by continuously flicking away at her. She'd put her paw in the air as if to say, "*Stop it. I don't like it*," though she tolerated it.

Afterward, I'd slick back Ryan's hair with a comb, and he'd laugh hilariously at the sensation of having it blow-dried. "Now you know how Katie feels when she gets her hair done!" I joked, also spraying some cologne on him, and patting him down with baby powder. (Katie stared at all this, jealous of the attention.)

Ryan, standing on top of the toilet seat, would look at himself in the mirror, making faces and dancing around. He'd then agilely step into his footie Power Rangers pajamas and head to the nearby couch in the living room and quickly fall asleep under a cotton blanket, Katie curled up in a ball next to him.

The third floor of our building was now a noisy one, with "the kid," as I nicknamed Ryan, and "the child," his canine companion, racing around from one apartment to another.

After five years of Katie being the center of attention, having Ryan on the floor was a complete and welcome novelty, "almost as much fun as raising a puppy," I joked to Pearl.

"And he can talk too," she laughed, as entranced by her new charge as I was.

Pearl loved taking on this new role, spoiling her "boy" by whipping up wickedly delicious dinners—tomato and Vidalia onion salads, paprika chicken cutlets, fried zucchini and squash, mashed potatoes with garlic, all of it topped off with home-baked apricot-and-plum tarts or chocolate pies.

"Mmmmm!" Ryan grinned merrily, only some of the food getting into his mouth, while the rest of it was smudged all over his face or on the floor.

Voracious Katie, perched on a green dining chair right next to his, would crane her neck to the right, lick the crumbs and ice-cream off Ryan's face, scour his empty plate, and then clean up the floor as well. Ryan giggled with delight at her industry.

On nights when Pearl made spaghetti, Ryan played one of his favorite games, holding each long strand of pasta way above Katie's head, just to torture her with suspense, then dropping it into her mouth, one piece at a time.

"That's my girl," said Pearl, "a very good vacuum cleaner."

Unlike Pearl, who reveled in babysitting and fussing over Ryan, Arthur was somewhat less enthusiastic. He was increasingly ailing physically, more susceptible to colds and respiratory infections than ever. He suffered from severe pain related to arthritis and shortness of breath caused by a heart condition.

Both challenges left him enervated and often depressed. So he mostly stayed indoors in his blue pajamas and plaid bathrobe, reading and watching TV, and, of course, snuggling with Katie.

Some mornings, Ryan would park himself in Arthur's twin bed, eager to watch his favorite cartoons. That's when the trouble began.

"The purple dinosaur!" Ryan demanded, announcing his preference for *Barney*. He also loved *Power Rangers*. But "Artur," as Ryan mispronounced his name, liked neither.

As John later remembered, "Arthur would get so mad when 'the kid' would watch cartoons in his bed because he wanted to watch the races."

Horses or cartoons—that was the question.

Sometimes Arthur did tolerate the dreaded cartoons, and watched absently as he fed his "girl" small chunks of apple as they stretched out together. Other times, he'd had enough.

"Stop changing channels, now!" shouted Arthur, taking the remote control back from Ryan, determined to have his way. And so it went, with the three-year-old and the eighty-three-year-old arguing over channels until Ryan was dismissed from the bedroom, dejected, angry, sometimes crying.

"Ryan, come to me," soothed Pearl, leading him over to the dining table where she began teaching him the basics of Go Fish and War, distracting him from cartoons. There they sat, playing cards while Katie watched, sometimes snapping up a card with her mouth and chewing on it. "Pa-Re-El!" Ryan shouted. "Tell her to stop!" And Katie would guiltily drop it.

Meanwhile, Arthur, feeling mild regret, would eventually come out of the bedroom holding up Katie's rubber ball, a peace offering. At this, my dog would immediately run to the front door and scratch it, asking to be let out.

Ryan would be in a much better mood—and off they all would go, Katie leading the way for a down-the-hall race with Ryan (with Arthur as referee).

"Now watch the ball," instructed Arthur, staring at his young charges. Both Katie and Ryan were on high alert, their eyes following his arm as he teased them with his warm-up. And then, he'd hurl the rubber ball to the far end of the hallway. Katie and Ryan took off in a flash, chasing after it.

With Ryan on her heels, and Pearl and Arthur cheering from their doorway, Katie galloped like the wind, each and every time faster than Ryan. She nimbly scooped the ball up with her mouth, and then, without stopping at the hall's end, looped back around for the return trip down to Arthur's door, where she dropped the ball at his feet, hoping he'd throw it again.

"Girlie, you're fast!" grinned Arthur, congratulating Katie with a biscuit.

"She got a head start," Ryan grumbled, racing to the door and demanding a rematch. So off they went again and again, until both boy and dog were completely winded.

Ryan was learning the art of being a good loser, while the "winner" promenaded in victory up and down the hall, having proved herself the alpha creature of the pack.

More than ever, our red-carpeted corridor was home base for Katie, her very own play space. To our seventeen neighbors along the hallway, who never socialized with one another, this public space meant little. But to Katie, it was her territory and frame of reference, the passageway connecting our three apartments.

I began to see that she instinctively used this hallway to glue us all together. She beckoned us up or down it with her head, in whatever direction suited her, and pulled us out of one apartment and into another. She was our canine traffic cop, a four-legged busybody telling us where she wanted us.

There she was at 6:00 p.m., racing down the hallway to pick up Ryan and herd him over to Pearl's for dinner. Then she'd make her way down to my apartment and scratch at my door, reminding me to come down as well.

After dinner, she'd race up and down the hall with Ryan again, with or without the ball, eventually herding him home to his apartment before returning to Pearl's to say good night— and then on home to me. She clocked more mileage than a car.

It was Katie—and only Katie—who could physically keep up with Ryan. "That's her job," joked John, "wearing Ryan out before bedtime."

On nights when "Daddy John" came home late from the newspaper, he'd often find Ryan stretched out on Pearl's living room couch, Katie on top of him, her paws protectively on his chest as the little boy slept.

And so, with her new friends down the hallway, Katie had expanded her role—not only a devoted companion to Arthur and Pearl, but also Ryan's enthusiastic playmate and fierce protector.

This last role was vividly displayed one day at our elevator when an aggressive eighty-five-pound Labrador retriever came along and barked at Ryan in a threatening manner. Katie, all of twenty-eight pounds, sprang into action, moving in front of Ryan and growling ferociously at the large dog as she cut him off, unafraid, seemingly ready to rip out his throat. The Lab backed away.

No dog was going to harm Ryan while she was around.

CHAPTER TWELVE

Gentlemen Prefer Blondes

Over the next year, we continued all our breakfasts, dinners, and impromptu visits up and down the hall, Katie gaining a few extra pounds despite her racing around until she was put on a special diet that no longer included Krispy Kreme donuts.

At Christmas, she got dressed up in a red coat and green hat and posed for pictures for Joe, our dog mentor, who always had a fantastic tree strung with pearls and glitter. He now proudly approved of the way Katie had matured and invited us twenty floors up for eggnog. Katie trotted into his kitchen and sat there patiently, waiting for a biscuit until she got one.

"Just one, Katie, and that's it!" he told her. Hearing the tone in his voice, she walked away from him after snatching it out of his hand.

As smart and determined as she was, Katie, like most dogs, wanted and needed structure and direction, and to this end, loved being talked to.

Right from the start, I got into the habit of having conversations with her, eye to eye, and I could tell that she clearly "understood" much of what I said. "Now, *listen* up, *child*, you're a *good* little dog, you are, but you have to learn your *manners*. *No biting*, no *scratching* your nails on the furniture, no getting up on the white couch, and no *accidents*. And if you're good, you'll get a *cookie* or a nice piece of *chicken*." Her ears immediately pricked up at these key words.

No, she didn't understand every word, but she did intuit the meaning of them from my tone, inflection, volume, and repetition of key phrases. Her vocabulary of about sixty words included *good*, *bad*, *no*, *eat*, *hungry*, *go out*, *go ahead* (meaning to do her business) *stay*, *sit*, *come*, and *beat it*.

If I asked, "*What are you doing*?" her head anxiously went up, as she stopped the offense. She also was well-acquainted with *cookie*, *treat*, *cake*, *coat*, *ball*, *keys*, *sock*, and *bone*, to mention just a few of her favorite things to eat or chew on.

And when she heard "get in your house," she always hightailed it back into her crate, happy to recline on her blue blanket while keeping a watchful eye on me.

With this arsenal of words at her command, and her ability to get the gist of my meaning, Katie was fully communicative.

Beyond her intelligence, her startling beauty was undeniable. Now age six, she had, according to a breeder who saw her, "one of the most beautiful cocker faces I've seen." In fact, a talented street artist I'd met in the shopping arcade at the World Financial Center drew a striking color pastel of Katie — capturing perfectly her soulful brown eyes flecked with gold, the long curly blond eyelashes, the pert black nose, and a face that was less square than most cockers', its contours feminine and expressive.

Her groomer, Betty, had created what we now called "the Katie cut," an unorthodox style for a cocker spaniel because it eliminated the long "skirt" that traditionally swept the ground on show dogs—the carpet sweeper style worn by Joe's Dinah. Instead, Betty cut Katie's silky coat close to the body.

"Girlfriend, get up here and give me five!" Betty commanded.

"This one's a devil," she told the groomer next to her. "Smart as a whip—but I've got her in line." Who had who "in line" I wasn't so sure.

Katie would merrily lift her paw and playfully hit Betty with it. She'd roll over on her stomach, paws straight into the air, manipulating Betty for a belly rub. But later on, she'd patiently lift each paw as directed, and hold it up as Betty trimmed around her nails. (During the entire two hours, Betty never stopped chattering away, and Katie seemed fascinated by every word.)

Betty would avoid shaving down Katie's head and instead left behind a fluffy "eyebrow," a fringe of hair, like an awning, just above her eyes. This made her look quite distinctive, though ridiculous when the brow got wet or sticky from food, which made it stand straight up. That always reminded me of the classic "hair gel" scene in the movie *There's Something About Mary*.

With her shampoo, crème rinse conditioner, and blow dry—not to mention her manicure and pedicure—Katie would emerge from each grooming a lustrous stunner. Sometimes when she held perfectly still, she almost looked unreal.

One day right after a grooming, Katie and I walked into Bergdorf Goodman, a Fifth Avenue department store that was dog friendly and lots of fun to browse in. She trotted into the elevator and we went up to the seventh floor ("Home") where they had bedsheets. While I was looking through the shelves, I told her, "Katie, SIT. Good girl. Now Staaaay." And she froze.

A moment later, a customer came by and I heard him ask a saleswoman, "How much is *that*?"

I turned around and this well-dressed businessman was pointing to *Katie*. He thought Katie was a stuffed animal!

When Katie then came to life and walked over to him, the startled man took in a breath, embarrassed.

"Oh, don't worry about it," I laughed. "She's flattered."

On the subway home, a young man in baggy pants and chains who looked like a rapper came into the car. I noticed him staring at Katie as she slept in my arms. He walked over to me: "How much?"

"Huh?"

"How much for the dog?" he asked.

Oh my God. "No, she's not for sale, sorry."

"I'll give you two hundred." I held onto her firmly, sensing a possible dog mugging.

Such are the perils of beauty (hers, not mine).

After that, especially as dogs weren't allowed in the subway except if they were in a kennel, we took taxis.

⟨🦴⟩

One evening after a dinner at Pearl's (Katie dragging her freshly groomed ears through a plate of spaghetti), a warming thought dawned on me, almost an epiphany.

For five years, we had been a strong band of four—Arthur, Pearl, Katie, and I. But with John and Ryan now so close to us, we had expanded to six, forming our own little "family" right in the building. It felt like we were now complete, just as close to one another as any biological family could be.

That night, as I lay in bed with Katie snoring softly next to me (exhausted from multiple races up and down the hall), I realized that I had never felt such deep contentment.

For much of my adult life, I'd been continually searching

Home sweet home: A view of Battery Park City, with the glass Winter Garden on the left, the marina in the middle, and our high-rise on the right. (Robert Simko / The Broadsheet)

From my apartment window, a never-ending parade of sailboats, up and down the Hudson. (Robert Simko / The Broadsheet)

Our first picture
together.

Katie moving in to her new
house surrounded by toys she
brought from the farm.

Wobbly on her feet, and homely, Katie strikes her first pose.

My new friends
and surrogate
grandparents,
Pearl and Arthur.

Pearl adored Katie and
burrowed in for hugs…

…while Arthur
taught her
proper table
manners.

Katie bonds with our new neighbors—John and his three-year-old son, Ryan.

Table time at Pearl's: Busybody Katie keeping a close watch on Ryan's ice cream.

Snuggling and watching cartoons.

Katie watching TV in her favorite chair.

Katie at work.

The nose knows: hiding, while keeping a tab on us.

Never missed a kernel.

Carrot cake for Katie's 7th, and me holding her back from devouring it all.

Tipsy Katie (after a bit of champagne!)

Her favorite party dress, held together with Velcro.

Katie in her prime, ruling the living room.

The *Family Circle* photo
shoot in Pearl's apartment.
(© 2000 ScottJonesPhotography.com)

Pearl, our hallway referee, just before
Katie and Ryan race.
(© 2000 ScottJonesPhotography.com)

Pearl just adored "the kid."
(© 2000 ScottJonesPhotography.com)

Granny's beloved Lee, who rescued her on September 11, 2001.

Valentine's Day, a few months after Pearl's 90th birthday.

The last picture of my beautiful Katie.

for a romantic relationship. However, I often wound up instead with false starts, mismatches, or relatively brief periods of connection followed by disappointment and frustration. I never quite got it right.

As a result, I'd often felt displaced, isolated, and oddly alone, even though I had many close friends and a supportive family. So the great void remained. I continued on my quest, always looking for that one relationship that, I hoped, would heal the emptiness I felt. It had never happened.

But everything changed when I turned in a new direction.

Suddenly, with no effort or planning, that empty space in my life was completely filled by my new "family." This was a huge shift that allowed me to open up in a way that I had never done before.

All the closeness, support, and connection I'd hoped for were right there for me—the nonstop action up and down the hall incredibly therapeutic.

Having spent so many years seeking the spotlight and a byline, I suddenly had nothing to prove. It was a real relief. And for the first time in many years, I felt as if I could actually *relax*.

True, I had lost my footing professionally, but what I had gained was a new appreciation of family.

Life now was like living in a college dorm, with doors constantly opening and closing, lots of crisscrossing in and out of each apartment, and all of us bonding ever more closely.

This didn't mean that I didn't date or strive for an intimate relationship. But in the meantime, our group provided a home for my heart, a steady source of security and love. It was a solid foundation upon which I could build an emotional life—with or without a mate.

And on nights when Ryan gave me a big hug and kiss good

night and Katie returned home to sleep, exhausted from the races, I realized how much I looked forward to the next day in a way that I never had before.

⌒

We all felt invigorated by Ryan's endless energy, which boosted everyone's spirits, day or night. I was amazed by the way he had bonded with Pearl so quickly, completely adoring and wanting to be with her as much as possible.

"In fact," John told me one night, "Pearl is probably *closer* to Ryan than most grandmothers would be to their grandchildren because she lives right down the hall, so she can see him on a *daily* basis." True enough. How many grandparents have that kind of access?

It was touching to see Ryan throw his arms around Pearl's neck, shyly giving her a kiss. "He's a great hugger — he's my boy," she'd beam.

Watching John's face at such moments, I could see the pleasure it gave him to expand his boy's world, and how gratified and supported he felt by Pearl's presence in his son's life.

Pearl was also making a difference in John's life. She had not only become a de facto grandmother to Ryan, but also an unofficial mom to John, giving him advice about everything from health and cooking to dating and child care.

"Pa-Re-El was telling me just today what to do about one of my bosses at work — that he should shove it!" John laughed, grateful for her unconditional support and grandmotherly pluck.

All in all, things could not have been better for all of us, except that Arthur was slowing down more and more. Although he was just as mentally acute as ever — a voracious reader of espionage thrillers and a devoted sports fan who could cite any score — his physical energy was flagging.

When I had first met him six years earlier, he was in and

out of the apartment throughout the day, taking long walks with Katie, chatting in the lobby with neighbors, and dropping into shops along our street.

But now, Arthur was mostly housebound, rarely leaving the house except for doctors' appointments, since he had difficulty walking due to arthritis and swelling in his feet.

Pearl had always been Arthur's caretaker, but now, more than ever, she watched over him, administered his medications, and took him to all his medical appointments. Other than visiting doctors, their outings became fewer and fewer.

More than ever, Pearl's dining table became our main meeting place, the center of our world. For Arthur especially, mealtime gave the day structure — and he looked forward to it immensely.

Pearl would go out to the farmers' market to scout for fresh vegetables and fruits, and by dinnertime the apartment was filled with mouthwatering aromas. By then, both Katie and Arthur were raring to go, emerging from their long afternoon naps in the bedroom with happy expectation.

While Arthur walked slowly, grumbling about his "charley horse" and pain in his feet, Katie ran ahead, jumping up on the green dining chair right next to his chair, her paws resting on the table as usual. Arthur then settled in, surveying the pot roast or paprika chicken.

And as the meal progressed, Katie kept an eagle eye on the proceedings. First she'd polish off her own dinner of dog food, eating it from the bowl set on the table. Then she'd beg Arthur for bits of chicken and corn, whimpering as she whacked his arm with her paw.

"Steady now, hold it girlie, stay!" he'd tease her, just as Ryan often did, lifting up a tasty morsel above Katie until he was ready to pop it into her mouth.

"Don't torture her," I'd say as Pearl looked on, satisfied that everybody appreciated her culinary effort.

As we all sat together, joined by Ryan and John, there was something poignant about watching Pearl and Arthur conversing about current events, neighborhood gossip, and Katie's antics, still engaged in lively dialogues after more than fifty years of marriage.

"Pearl, dear," Arthur would say, gesturing for her to pass the potatoes, "tell everyone about that honeymoon meal we had in Atlantic City," to which Pearl would vividly recount the greatest clam chowder and stuffed flounder she'd ever tasted. "Atlantic City wasn't all glitzed up back then," Arthur chimed in, pointing to the couple's favorite photo perched up on their mahogany liquor cabinet—the black-and-white shot of them on the boardwalk.

As they chatted, I had plenty of time to observe the little things that told the entire story of the love they shared. Pearl would get up after dinner and stand behind his chair, putting both of her hands firmly on each of his shoulders, and massaging them. He'd lean back and close his eyes, comforted by her touch. Other times, he'd lightly touch her arm and stroke it, compliment her on dinner, and politely ask for dessert in the living room. Later on, they'd watch basketball and baseball together on the TV, cheering for the New York Knicks or Yankees.

Pearl was genuinely interested in what Arthur had to say—even when he repeated himself. Over dinner, he'd often launch into one of his old (and corny) jokes for the umpteenth time, his energetic (and dry) delivery making it new again. One of his favorites was his "matchmaker" story, which he'd cart out for anyone new who came to dinner.

"A marriage broker offered Morty a beautiful young girl, a real prize, to be his wife," began Arthur. "But Morty was stubborn. 'I'm a businessman,' Morty argued. 'Before I buy material from a mill, I look at swatches. So before I get married, I gotta have a sample also.'

"The broker had no choice but to relay the message to the girl. 'He says he has to know exactly what he's buying and insists on a sample.'

"'Listen,' the girl replied, 'I'm also good at business. A sample I don't give. But, I *will* give him references!'" Arthur would then erupt in uproarious laughter and Pearl would join in heartily.

And on it went, with Arthur's high spirits carrying us all along.

But then, a shadow was cast over our world in the fall of 1994, when Arthur was hospitalized with pneumonia. Weeks before, he'd been coughing, unable to shake off a bad cold. Increasingly depressed, he seemed more detached than usual, even spending less and less time with Katie, who sat on top of him every chance she got.

Pearl was very upset and went to the hospital every morning, as soon as visiting hours began. And I often went with her, wanting to see Arthur and give her the support she needed. She was so stressed out. All of her life, Pearl had been Arthur's only caretaker, as much his mother as his wife, and she'd done an excellent job of it. But now, Arthur's condition was out of her control.

On one of our visits, Arthur was disoriented, tortured by the intravenous tubes running in and out of him, including a feeding tube down his throat.

"Please," he whispered in a raspy voice, firmly gripping my wrist, "cut the tubes with a penknife!" I knew he wasn't thinking correctly, and it broke my heart to see him this way. He was in so much pain and wanted out of it. "Please, do it!" he begged.

Afterward, Pearl and I were both shaken and walked across the street from New York Hospital to a little Chinese restaurant and shared lunch as we frequently did. We talked quietly about Arthur's worsening condition and I saw something in Pearl's eyes that I'd never seen before — fear.

At nights, Arthur's chair was empty at our "family dinners." We missed the deep sound of his voice and his common-sense remarks, even his complaints about the cartoons. Every night, Ryan asked about "Artur's" condition. Katie obviously missed him too, as she napped alone on his lounge chair, looking forlorn.

Then, one freezing day in early January 1995, Pearl went to the hospital alone to see Arthur. Late that afternoon, she knocked on my door. When I opened it, she was so pale.

For the first time ever, this strong, proud woman — the stoic, always upbeat matriarch of our family — was crushed, tears filling her eyes as we embraced.

I knew.

"Oh, no...I'm so sorry."

"They tried to save him, more than once," she whispered, "but it was too late. And...." She choked on her words as I led her over to my couch.

Pearl and Arthur had been married for *fifty-nine* years, and now Arthur was gone, at age eighty-five.

"We almost made it to sixty," Pearl smiled. She sat down on the couch and gazed out of the window while absently holding Katie close.

We were all bereft. Ryan was too young to fully understand what had happened, though he cried when John explained that Arthur was in heaven and was never coming back. "Never?!" he asked.

For weeks afterward, Katie moped around Pearl's

apartment, aware of Arthur's absence and mournfully lying on his favorite chair, almost as if guarding it for him as she slept on his bathrobe, which held his scent. Without him, there was a deafening silence in apartment 3C.

The next day, we all accompanied Pearl to the cemetery up in Westchester County in the most atrocious weather imaginable. It was stormy and depressing with teeming rain, high winds, and mud slides. Pearl almost lost her footing as we made our way down a hill to the family plot. I held onto her left arm while Ryan tightly gripped her right hand, and John held a giant umbrella over all of us. Katie sank into the wet ground, the mud covering most of her paws, but she soldiered on and sat at attention as Arthur's coffin was lowered.

Amid all of us humans, there was Arthur's canine companion, her face soaked with the rain, wanting to be part of her "pack," through thick and thin.

When we got back home, Pearl was exhausted.

"That," she told me over a cup of steaming tea, "was the worst day of my life." Saying good-bye to Arthur was the only time I ever saw Pearl cry.

Chapter Thirteen

"Ready, Set, Go!"

O n a warm spring afternoon in 1996, a familiar yellow school bus, filled with talkative six- to nine-year-olds, pulled up to our complex, its red lights blinking as it stopped in front of the local ice-cream and bagel shop.

Together with many of the waiting moms and dads, Pearl was there too, right on time for her 3:00 p.m. pickup—the highlight of her day.

She was dressed in sensible black lace-up shoes, a gray tweed skirt, and a blue windbreaker, her thick mane of hair blowing in the breeze.

Katie was also eagerly waiting at the stop, sitting at attention as the door of the bus opened. She scrutinized each of the kids coming down the steps, searching nervously for six-year-old Ryan.

And then there he was—giggling wildly with a friend as he jumped off the bus, outfitted in a denim jacket, blue jeans, and red sneakers, a blue Power Rangers backpack falling off his shoulders.

Katie dashed forward and nearly knocked Ryan over, jumping up on her hind legs to greet him.

"Hi, Katie girl," he smiled, bending down to affectionately stroke her head, then running into Pearl's arms. She enveloped him in a huge hug.

"Graaaaanny!" he boomed, "this is for *you*." He handed Pearl a little ceramic dish he'd made that day in arts and crafts.

"Thank you, sweetheart. How was your day?" she asked, getting back a quick "fine" before the boy skipped ahead, with Katie trailing after him. The two raced home together.

Somewhere along the line, Pearl's nickname Pa-Re-El had morphed into Granny, stretched out as *Graaaaanny*, the longer the better. If we wanted to tease Pearl, we called her *Oldest Granny*, which drew a smile, or just *Oldest*, which elicited a mock frown.

And Pearl wasn't the only member of our group who got a stretched-out nickname. By this point in time, Katie's moniker, "the child," was now pronounced "*chaaa-aellll-d*," which Ryan repeated in a singsong over and over again with glee.

"Hello, chaaa-aellll-d!" he giggled, rubbing her head. "You good or bad?"

That all depended.

For example, when Pearl used Katie's nickname, it was usually to underline a point. Upon returning home, I'd typically ask her, "So, how was my sweet little chaaa-aellll-d today?" to which she'd enumerate her various infractions—stealing food (scarfing down Pearl's pound cake, one of her favorites), having accidents, pulling apart a sock, you name it.

"Your sweet little child isn't so sweet today," opined Granny, shuffling Katie to the door with her feet and laughing, always forgiving of her canine charge.

Likewise, even with the mayhem that Ryan sometimes created, which included overflowing her bathtub or splattering finger paint on her floor, Oldest seemed happier than I'd ever seen her, though she never said it out loud.

In the year and a half since Arthur had died, I'd seen a gradual change in Pearl. At first, she was disoriented and profoundly sad, as anyone with such a devastating loss would be, and she mostly stayed at home, sorting through Arthur's clothing and giving most of it away to the Salvation Army.

But after a few months, she seemed to rebound quickly from her loss and didn't often talk about it. Instead, she began taking advantage of her new freedom. She spent more time with women friends in the building—shopping with them, talking on the phone, and attending neighbor-to-neighbor teas.

Every morning, she and I had breakfast together, where we mostly talked about Katie, while in the afternoons, Pearl would roam Battery Park on long walks with her "girl." I also drew Pearl into my activities more than ever, inviting her to movies, plays, dinners, and parties.

But more than anything, it was Ryan who was the key to Pearl's recovery from losing Arthur. His adorable presence was like a powerful elixir to Pearl. It energized her and gave her new purpose, providing grand distractions and deep affection. Her world now revolved around *him*—though she would deny it.

"He's a brat!" she'd protest good-naturedly, ordering Ryan out of the house and into the hall for soccer practice after one of his high kicks nearly smashed her favorite white china pitcher. He bragged that he had control of the ball. "And I've got control of you!" she countered.

With pride, she'd tell her friends that "the kid" was undeniably athletic and the cutest little boy imaginable (which he really was, with those dimples and unruly cowlick).

And so, with John at work each day, Oldest had taken on her babysitting role with relish, picking Ryan up every afternoon and taking him to her home for cookies, milk, and more.

She *was* Ryan's grandmother. She truly was. And it made me happy to see how much Pearl was reinvigorated by the closeness to Ryan and her new responsibility. She focused on her young charge with total devotion.

As John later reflected, "With Arthur gone, Pearl took Ryan on as her life's project—her *mission*."

"Most days when Ryan gets off the bus," Pearl told us proudly one night, "he runs right over and hugs me.

"His friends just stand there looking kind of cockeyed," she said, "and I ask them: 'Do any of *you* have a Granny?' They shake their heads no and come over to me. So I hug them all!"

"Do they like it?" John asked.

"Yes, they do."

It touched my heart to see the satisfaction in Pearl's eyes as she related this, knowing how she had lost her own chance for motherhood decades earlier. At last, she had found a child that loved and needed her.

⊂⊃

So Pearl was now Ryan's number one babysitter, the main female presence in his life, reliably stepping in for John anytime he was at work, at a meeting, or on a date. (Katie acted as Pearl's energetic aide-de-camp.)

"Wednesday is *my* day," Pearl announced at first, though her after-school babysitting role soon expanded to most any day. She helped Ryan with his homework, packed up his Power Rangers lunch box for the next day, whipped up chicken or meat loaf for dinner, and rewarded him at dessert time with her graham-cracker-crust chocolate pie (or spoiled him with Krispy Kreme doughnuts).

Dessert time also now included Ben & Jerry's Chunky Monkey—banana ice cream with fudge chunks and walnuts. You could always depend on Katie to lick Ryan's bowl clean. "No need for a dishwasher with her around," quipped Granny, wary that Katie never ate any of the chocolate chunks that were so bad for dogs.

Once, Pearl was spraying whipped cream on Ryan's ice cream when Katie dove into the bowl, her nose instantly covered with the white topping. When Ryan objected, Granny spritzed *him* on the face with the cream, Katie merrily licked it off his nose. And so it went.

"But Granny," John told me one day, "is no pushover and she won't stay up with 'the kid' past eleven o'clock—so I better damn well be home by then."

"And if you're not," Pearl scolded, "that's your problem, not mine."

When this happened, she usually turned Ryan over to me. That meant that I'd literally pick him up and carry him—sound asleep in my arms—from Pearl's to my apartment and place him on my living room couch next to Katie until John got back. Later, John would scoop him up and carry him home. Through it all, Ryan never woke up.

But first thing in the morning, Ryan was right back at Granny's door, ready for some fun. This twosome, seventy-eight years apart, could be heard giggling for hours at Pearl's dining table as they talked about school and played cards together. "Granny really knows how to play," Ryan told John, "and she usually beats me." Sometimes I'd find them finger painting at the table or putting together a model airplane.

Ryan was intently curious about everything in Pearl's world. One day, he poked his head into her bedroom closet as she pulled out Arthur's coin and stamp collections, along with a silver stopwatch that Arthur had used when judging track meets at Madison Square Garden. Ryan marveled at the heavy timepiece. I could see Pearl getting emotional as she held it in her hand. "One day," she promised, "when you're older, I'll make sure you have this."

Sometimes when I came into her apartment, Ryan would be on the couch with his feet propped up on Granny's lap, Katie next to him, as Pearl read him one of the Curious George books or taught him how to do a crossword puzzle. At other times, Pearl, who loved gardening, would show Ryan how to pot a plant or properly water the dozens of blooms set along her windowsill.

"Don't overwater," she instructed as Ryan flooded a small plant, though he soon got the hang of it, enjoying the process of filling the water can and using it.

Ryan was also interested in Pearl's collection of old vinyl LPs. "Choose one," she'd smile, and a few minutes later I'd find them singing and dancing together to Frank Sinatra or Dean Martin, or to the soundtrack of *My Fair Lady*.

You never knew what you might find going on in 3C!

At Halloween, Granny surprised Ryan by wearing a monster mask when he trick-or-treated at her door.

At Thanksgiving, she stuffed him with turkey.

At Christmas, she reached up to the top of the tree to position the star.

On July Fourth, she took him outside to watch the fireworks—lighting up the sky and the Statue of Liberty just down the river in the harbor.

And on his birthday in August, she helped blow out that last stubborn candle, wiping chocolate off his face.

In short, when it came to being a grandmother, Pearl was everything that a boy could ask for—and more.

Pearl, who took special pride in the meals she prepared, also began teaching Ryan the basics of cooking, starting with scrambled eggs and French toast. "This is how you break the eggs," she explained as he looked on at the frying pan with a spatula in his hand. (It was poignant seeing this eighty-four-year-old patiently teaching a six-year-old.) Katie attempted to push him out of the way with her paws, wanting to stand next to Pearl and capture any morsel that fell to the floor, but Ryan nudged her back with his foot.

Around this time, I also got on a cooking kick—and Pearl was my "taster" down the hall. At first, I attempted to bake some of the desserts my grandmother had made, plus others I'd seen on the Food Network. As soon as they were fresh out of the oven, I'd bring my attempts down the hall for table tests.

"Oh, my," Pearl would grimace. "Maybe you should take a class." (Most of my creations found their way into Pearl's wastebasket, sorry to say.)

But I persisted, and after watching Martha Stewart's show for months (she made everything look so easy and I liked her calm, detailed approach), I was inspired to go out and buy a professional mixer and the right pans and utensils. Everything was gleaming new.

"Granny, can you come over? I'm about to try out Julia Child's pound cake with vanilla glacé…" And Pearl was down the hall in a flash, standing next to me. She sifted the flour (warning me not to add the dry ingredients too quickly into the wet ones), measured out the baking powder and vanilla, leveled in the cake batter, and later helped me mix up the frosting and spread it. Standing side by side brought back such fond memories of Nana, whom I missed—so I treasured this kitchen time with Pearl. Katie followed our every move.

Sometimes the cakes were complete flops—over- or

underdone—and taken right down to the garbage chute. Other times they were tasty but lopsided, and we gave them away to the doorman downstairs (who I heard fed them to the dogs in the building). Once in a while, the result was perfect, and Katie helped us polish it all off in an evening.

One night, I was convinced I'd mastered a recipe and couldn't understand why Granny spit out her slice. "You put *SALT* into it instead of sugar!" she scowled, scraping it into the wastebasket—once again.

After two hours of baking and frosting, I would be tired, while Pearl would look as fresh as ever.

Indeed, though Granny had years on me, she had more stamina (and a healthier back) than I did. There she was, lugging laundry to the utility room, mopping floors, trudging to the bus stop for a shopping expedition, taking Ryan to play dates or soccer practice, or going out on long hikes on the Esplanade with Katie and her "boy," showing them both off as grandmothers do.

Ryan was also interested in showing *Granny* off. He took her photograph to his art teacher at school. And a week later he proudly brought home a striking pen-and-ink drawing that he thereafter kept in his bedroom. In it, the artist had captured Pearl's homespun expression—her plump cheeks with dimples, her high forehead, the unruly mane of hair, and her expressive eyes, that were, humorously, hooded with the extra skin that comes with age. Not the girly type, Pearl's idea of makeup was putting on some lipstick for a wedding. Other than that, she wore none at all.

"Half the time," John smiled in later years, "she looked a little like something from a Marx Brothers movie with that wild hair." But that only made her more lovable. To me, Pearl was as basic as bread, not fancy or primped in any way.

When it came to taking care of Ryan, Pearl wasn't particularly strict, though she kept a watchful, amused eye on everything that "the kid" and Katie did. From the bedroom doorway in her apartment, she once caught them eating bagels together in bed, Katie licking cream cheese off Ryan's lips. Then Katie snoozed on top of Ryan, loudly snoring, as he watched cartoons.

When Ryan had a friend over for a playdate, Katie ran around the apartment as they played War, circling the boys. And at night, Katie would even submit to bubble baths with Ryan, her face becoming all sudsy as he rinsed her with little cups of water.

After Ryan's bath, there was always time for a final race down the hallway, with Pearl acting as referee. Unlike the days when Arthur would throw Katie's rubber ball, we now had running contests with no ball at all. To make the race fair, I'd line Katie and Ryan up on an imaginary starting line right in front of Pearl's front door, holding my arm out to keep them both positioned, like horses.

"Now *stay*, Katie," I told her, though she sometimes "jumped the gun," trying to gain an advantage over Ryan.

"She's cheating!" Ryan hollered, scowling.

"Shhhhh," exclaimed Pearl. "Get with it, Katie."

I'd call Katie back and she cooperatively lined up again.

Then Pearl made her announcement: *"Ready...Set... Goooooooo!"*

Ryan and Katie galloped wildly down to the end of the hallway and then back again to Pearl, a blur of energy. More often than not, Katie was the triumphant winner ("she cheated again," Ryan would mope), her head held high in the air and her tongue hanging out of her mouth. As usual, she'd promenade in a victory lap back up the hall before hightailing it back to Pearl's for a reward.

These races got to be such a hit on our floor that several of the neighbors would open their doors and cheer from the sidelines. "Go Ryan!" shouted one college student, encouraging "the kid" to overtake my dog, while Freda, my across-the-hall neighbor, would root for Katie. One night, five doors opened, everyone laughing and cheering as Katie swept down the hall, the winner yet again. Ryan was looking down, vowing to beat "the child" next time, as Katie licked his face, unaware of how she'd irritated her little friend.

After three or four races, it was time to tuck Ryan into "his" bed in Pearl's bedroom. The boy put his arms around Granny for a hug good night while Katie crawled in next to him, her head nuzzled on his shoulder.

"She licks my face and kisses me a lot," he told Granny, as he yawned.

"That's because she loves you. Now go to sleep."

On nights like these, Ryan and Katie were in seventh heaven—and so was Granny.

CHAPTER FOURTEEN

The Accident

During the darkest days of my nonworking years when my back was at its worst, there were times when I literally couldn't walk.

It was quite a turnaround for me. It wasn't so long before that I was jetting from coast to coast for interviews; now I was literally crawling from the bedroom to the bathroom.

"Pearl, can you come down?"

"I'll be right there," she clipped, hanging up the phone. And within minutes, with Katie skipping merrily behind her, Pearl was down the hall to my apartment ready to offer a helping hand, whether it was changing the bed linens, bringing in groceries, or helping me up from the floor and back to the bed.

It was pretty ironic. I was sometimes laid up with back spasms and pain that made it difficult, or impossible, to straighten up or walk while my much older friend, Pearl, was in excellent health, coming to my rescue when I most needed her.

Katie, Pearl, John, and Ryan were all like a tonic, dramatically lifting my spirits and giving me a *reason* to recover from what seemed like an intractable problem that had led me to feeling severely depressed.

In fact, I was, at times, so down that I went back to sleep after taking Katie out for her first walk of the day. On Tuesdays, when Ramon arrived, he'd let himself in and walk into the bedroom, sitting down on the bed.

"Good morning!" he'd say, knowing how badly I felt. And as Katie jumped in his lap to say hi, he'd gently pat my leg, his voice soothing.

"I tried to cheer you up," he later told me. "But it was terrible. You'd stay in bed and say, 'just clean around me,' and that's what I did."

Granny, who adored Ramon, would often stop in for a visit.

"You're going to be just fine," she opined, bringing in matzo ball soup on a tray and sitting on the bed as we chatted.

"This is good for colds, not backs," I joked.

"Honey," she laughed, "this is good for *everything*. Eat it before Katie does."

Indeed, Queen Katie would be sprawled casually on top of me, regal on the green bedspread, eyeing that soup like a hawk. She was, of course, oblivious to anything out of the ordinary in terms of my mobility.

Truth be told, my dog *liked* me in bed—the more time in there the better. She would slap my arm with her paw when she was hungry. When she wanted to be combed out, she'd retrieve the brush from a straw basket I kept on the floor. It was as if she was saying, "*Dad, c'mon, I need my ears done.*" She liked them untangled and fluffy.

"Your girl looked like a drowned rat on the Esplanade," Pearl pronounced one day when she and Katie came in from walking in heavy rain. "Dry her off," she ordered, throwing me a bath towel.

"*Yeah, Dad, get moving,*" the "child" motioned, pushing her wet head into my stomach. Then, Granny would pull out the hair dryer and Katie would patiently stand on the bed until she was perfectly dry.

Some days after school, Ryan would burst into my bedroom to see Katie and me. He would throw himself on the bed, give us a hug, and show me what he'd been up to that day in school.

"Beat it, off, off," exclaimed Ryan, as Katie tangled herself in the covers, snooping into his backpack for leftover snacks.

Having Katie and Ryan wrestling together completely distracted me from myself, which was the best medicine of all.

At nights, when John got home, Pearl would bring an entire dinner for everyone into my bedroom. "Let's have a picnic," she'd suggest. "Your bed is the table, so you'd better get ready for us."

And promptly at seven, right after Pearl watched the evening news, there we were, Katie and Ryan positioned on the bed and John and Pearl sitting on chairs nearby, all of us digging into Granny's chicken cutlets.

"Like the salad?" she asked, savoring the fresh vegetables that she had scooped up earlier at our nearby farmers' market, "for half the price of the supermarket," she noted proudly.

"Eat your tomatoes," she told Ryan—who slipped more than one of them into Katie's mouth when Pearl wasn't looking.

"I saw that," she snapped. "No dessert until you eat them."

"But they're gone!" Ryan protested.

"Now they're back!" laughed John, plunking his own tomatoes on Ryan's plate.

And then, at dessert time, Pearl brought out a homemade pear tart, as always, giving Katie her own slice on a plate. Ryan would carefully put a piece of the tart on the fork and hold it up for Katie as she delicately pulled the cake off without ever biting into the fork, getting every crumb.

Katie was now a mature girl of nearly eight, no less bouncy than before but definitely bossier, and quite definite about what she wanted and when.

For example, even when I was trapped in bed, she'd retrieve a sock and jump up on the bed and throw it at me, ready for tug-of-war. "You hit me in the face with it!" I objected one day. She just stared at me obstinately, determined to play.

You either complied or she would rip the sock to shreds on her own.

Having built on her TV-remote skills at Granny's, she now liked grabbing the remote control away from me as well, pushing down on it to change channels until she hit one she liked.

In the winter, after she came in from a walk, she liked having her paws washed off with warm paper toweling, something I'd done since she was a puppy. She'd either trot into the bathroom and sit there, waiting, or grab a roll of towels from the bathroom and bring it to me, dropping it for me on the bed.

Talk about smart.

Katie's antics, our family dinners, and Pearl's caretaking made even the worst of days the best of times. And not coincidentally, my health was slowly improving.

Thanks to physical therapy, massage, and a great chiropractor, I was back to taking long walks, swimming, and even riding a bike.

"Hey, Glenn P!" shouted Ryan one brisk October day, outfitted in his yellow bike helmet, headed for a ride on the Esplanade. "My Dad and I are going out…want to come?"

Yes, I did! And from that point on, whenever I could, I was back on my bike tooling along the Hudson River, with Katie on a leash, trotting from behind. Ryan led the way, talking nonstop to "the child," telling her to stop pulling on the leash, though she was more interested in snooping on the ground for crumbs. It was a fun time—and a great relief to be outside again.

One morning in March 1996, Katie was, as always, snuggled up against my chest, her long ears draped across my arm. Listening to her snore contentedly under my down comforter was such a consoling, peaceful way to begin the day.

In the midst of a happy dog dream, she'd woken me up with the swat of her tail against my stomach—her brown eyes sealed shut by those long blond eyelashes.

Held at bay by the canine snooze was, of course, the less enviable part of being a dog owner—the walk outside. Even on such an unseasonably warm day as this one, Katie, who no doubt heard the wind whistling outside, resisted the inevitable.

"C'mon, Blondie, let's go," I said, nudging her awake by giving her a kiss on the nose. She opened one eye and then closed it again.

"*It's too early*," she seemed to tell me, burrowing deeper under the sheets to escape. "*I need some shut-eye!*"

I insisted. Katie marshaled her energy and we were up and out along the Hudson River within five minutes, walking briskly.

It seemed that my disability days were finally coming to an end, though I still found myself wrestling with morning depression.

On that March day, the "down" feeling was palpable, like a heavy weight pressing on me.

Despite the many blessings in my life, I sometimes still only focused on what I *didn't* have—namely a job. I had never really recovered from the loss of that newspaper position, while the physical problems I'd experienced had cut into my self-confidence and left me feeling defective and inadequate.

Much as I used to complain about the daily pressures of a full-time job, structure was golden for me, and I sorely missed saying good morning to colleagues, sharing jokes, having lunch dates, racing around to interviews, and sticking to a tight schedule.

Without all that, what was I now? What was my purpose?

"Snap out of it!" exclaimed Granny that morning at breakfast, using one of her favorite expressions, a line taken from the Cher movie *Moonstruck*, which she loved. "You've got your girl, me, John, and the kid, and things could be a lot worse."

Pearl had some of the same no-nonsense qualities as the heroine of that film. Both were pragmatic and fiery, stoic and stubborn. No matter what she said, I found her presence put things right into perspective.

"Now pass the butter."

By midafternoon, when I left for my weekly therapy appointment, the wind had dramatically died down, so I decided to ride my bike the three miles uptown, setting out with just one thing purposely left behind—a bike helmet. I hated wearing it because having my head enclosed felt claustrophobic.

The effectiveness of therapy, for me, was transitory, its benefit vanishing a few hours after I left the office. It was far less effective than Granny. Today was no exception.

After the appointment, now heading home on the bike, I remember feeling slightly lightheaded, as I was getting over a cold. I considered putting my bike into a taxi, but then dismissed the idea.

I knew the route home so well that I hardly paid any attention as I automatically rode south on Seventh Avenue, then west on Christopher Street toward the Hudson River, and made the final approach from city traffic to the bike path along the deserted river's edge.

The pavement here was crumbling, with shards of broken glass everywhere. Pedaling quickly and then making a sharp left turn, I had nearly escaped traffic and reached the bike path when I suddenly hit a deep crack in the cement.

Without any warning, I went flying over the handlebars, so quickly that I had no chance to break the fall with my hands. It was like being fired out of a cannon and catapulted through the air in a flash. I saw it all in slow motion, aware of my trajectory but helpless to stop it.

A second later, I landed on the cement with a crunch, flat on my face—my nose, lips, forehead, and sunglasses smashed into the cracked cement and broken glass.

There was total silence. I couldn't move, and didn't even try to. It was as if I'd accidentally walked into a wall of glass. In my peripheral vision, I could see my fallen bike in a heap nearby. My face felt numb and wet, and my knees were burning. I lay still.

Then someone appeared by my side. I saw just his feet.

"Dude! You okay?"

"Yeah," I kind of groaned, "but I can't move," I told him, attempting to push myself up.

"Don't do that…just don't move." He called 911 and stayed with me, putting his hand gently on my arm. Flat on my face, I never did see his face. But I felt his concern. And later, as the events of the day unfolded, I would understand that this man's simple act of kindness was the beginning of the end of my depression.

Within a few minutes an ambulance from St. Vincent's Hospital appeared, siren blaring. I remember EMS workers placing a brace over my neck—with the expectation that I might have broken it—then lifting me from the pavement and putting me onto the stretcher.

As I was being rolled into the ambulance, I pulled from my pocket my business card and asked the man who'd helped me if he would ride my bike home.

"I'll take care of it, don't you worry about it," he told me. And off we went.

❦

When we reached the hospital, all sense of time was suspended. Although the emergency room was bustling with doctors, nurses, and patients, I saw the scene around me as if the sound was turned off.

As it turned out, there was a deep gash across my forehead requiring eighteen stitches and another one under my nose that had ripped my lip apart. On top of that, my nose was broken, both knees were bleeding, there were contusions all over my face, and my left eye was black and swollen, nearly closed.

A nurse came by offering to telephone someone who could come to the hospital to support me. I gave her the office number of one of my all-time best friends, Michael, a brilliant twenty-nine-year-old lawyer who also happened to be blessed with a riotous sense of humor. He could see the irony in anything, and could always make me laugh. I really needed that now. Michael was a once-in-a-lifetime find, the kind of friend you hope for. He was close to my family; adored Katie, Granny, and Ryan; showed up at all our parties; and even helped me with legal matters.

When Michael got to the hospital, he had to wait for "visiting time" in the ER, which was the last ten minutes of every hour. At the appropriate time, a nurse led him back into the ER and he walked right past my bed.

"I would never have recognized you," he later told me. "Your face was a bloody pulp. You looked like you'd been knocked out in a boxing match. And you were moaning, this slow steady groan of unabated pain."

Up until then, I had remained pretty calm. But when an orderly wheeled me into the X-ray room, with Michael following, I pretty much lost it, all defenses down. Just at the moment they transferred me from the portable cot to the X-ray table, I began to cry and couldn't stop.

I wasn't just upset about my accident. It was as if all the emotions I'd felt about what had happened to my career and health were amplified and brought to the surface, bursting out of me in one convulsive, and embarrassing, sob.

My next thought was "Granny."

Michael called her on the phone, explained the situation, and she raced into a taxi and was at the hospital in fifteen minutes.

"Glenn," she quipped, pulling aside the curtain and walking into the cubicle. "I leave you alone for an hour and you wind up in a place like this!" That was Granny.

She calmly proceeded over to my bedside to get a better look, holding on her arm a large cloth canvas shopping bag, the one she used at the farmers' market.

"Honestly," Michael later said. "Granny was more composed than I was. I'd never seen anyone look the way you did, and I was pretty shaken up."

But Pearl, outwardly calm, wasn't so unaffected by what was happening. She was actually quite upset seeing me in this condition, but she never let it show.

"I brought something to cheer you up," she said, rifling into her bag.

"Oh, Granny, I'm not up for any cookies right now."

"I've got something much better than that," she smiled. And there, popping out from under a pink towel was *Katie*! Pearl had smuggled her into the hospital, past the ER nurses, using the same technique I had used when sneaking Katie into the *Daily News* building years earlier.

"She never moved when I told her to stay quiet," said Pearl proudly, lifting Katie up onto my hospital cot. "I guess those obedience lessons paid off."

Never had I been as happy to see my dog as I was that day. She tried to lick my face, but that was impossible. So Granny held her steady, and she soon fell asleep next to me, hiding under the sheet. No doctor was the wiser.

Michael stood guard, remaining on the lookout for any ER doctors or nurses (who would certainly seek the immediate ouster of a canine intruder) while Pearl and I talked quietly. For the rest of my ER stay, Katie stayed under the sheet or hidden in the bag, evading eviction, as Granny talked into the bag, perhaps mistaken for someone with senile dementia!

Blessings were piling up. The first one was the man who discovered me on the ground. Then there was the rapid response of the ambulance, the care of the nurses, and now two of my closest friends were sitting by my side.

Next, a young plastic surgeon arrived offering a big smile. "We're going to fix you up—and you'll have no scars left behind," he assured me, though I wasn't prepared for what followed. After cleaning up my face and stitching up the cuts, the doctor explained that he was going to reset my nose *without* anesthesia.

"But why?" I asked, dreading any more pain.

"We can't give anesthesia when we believe a patient may have sustained a concussion or a neck injury—so you're going to have to bite the bullet and trust me. We'll get through it quickly, I promise."

As he manipulated my nose with his instruments, I heard a loud crack as he was resetting the bone. I was in agony, in the most physical pain I'd ever experienced. Adding to the drama was blood spraying all over the wall.

"When the doctor reset your nose, you let out the most intense shriek," said Michael. "That kind of pain was just unfathomable to me."

And then, to my amazement, an hour after my face was bandaged and my nose filled with packing, the plastic surgeon announced, "You can go home."

"He can go where?" asked Michael, astonished by this.

"We can't keep him in the hospital. He's fine. But if his nose starts bleeding again during the night, call the ER."

So at 9:00 p.m., six hours after it all began, I was released from the hospital, barely able to walk. But that's exactly what I did, supported on each arm by Michael and Pearl. A second before the door closed behind us, Katie jumped out of her shopping bag and the last thing I remember is the shocked expression of the nurse. Too late now!

⬭

The taxi ride home to Battery Park City was a quiet one, each of us lost in our own thoughts. Michael and Pearl were incredible friends that night. In fact, they were much more than that: They were *family*.

And it wasn't just that they showed up and stayed with me. Anyone could do that. They really *cared*—and I would never forget it.

That night, with my defenses down, I realized just how much I loved them, and how that feeling was so readily returned to me. A sense of thankfulness filled me up. Finally, I understood something that I had read long ago—that *a grateful heart can never be a depressed one*. The two emotions are antithetical.

Holding onto both Pearl and Michael, I made my way slowly down the hall toward my apartment door.

Small acts of kindness continued. Michael helped pull off my bloody T-shirt without disturbing the bandages on my face. Pearl pulled back the covers and propped up some pillows. Katie jumped up on the bed and nestled next to me.

John, who had been at work and unable to come to the hospital, brought Ryan down the hallway. Both of them were anxious to see me.

"You look bad—like Monster Man," exclaimed Ryan, intrigued as only a child could be by my swollen face. He was completely unfazed by it, happy to lie on the bed next to me, together with Katie.

"Pip," as John sometimes called me, "you won't be going out on dates anytime soon!" he laughed.

It was Oscar night, so Michael flipped on the TV, and we all watched Mira Sorvino win Best Supporting Actress for *Mighty Aphrodite*.

Lying in bed, surrounded by everyone, I never felt more at peace. I also knew that I was lucky. The entire day had been a lesson in gratitude. The depressed person of that morning was gone. Maybe human nature works that way: You don't really know how fortunate you are until all that you take for granted is threatened.

That's why the accident was a gift, leading to an epiphany that literally snapped me out of my ungrateful, depressed state of mind. It forced me to count my blessings—the people (and the dog) in my life.

On this night, I especially appreciated Katie's upbeat love for all of us, reflected in her countless runs up and down the hall, herding us together.

I took in the happy bounce of her gait, her curious nose, her exuberant smile, and her tongue hanging out with pleasure.

Once again, even in the ER, she had helped pull me through a difficult time, consoling, entertaining, and immeasurably enhancing the quality of all our lives.

That night, just before I went to sleep, Granny brought in some apple juice with a straw and sat next to me without talking. She looked out the window at the river, stroking Katie's head in a slow rhythm.

Soon, she went back down the hall, though she made sure that John looked in on me throughout the night.

And then, with the heat turned to high and Katie next to me just as she'd been that morning, I drifted off to sleep, ending my day in an infinitely better place than I ever could have imagined.

CHAPTER FIFTEEN

Party Girls

The next five years whirled by quickly, a string of dinners, shared holidays, and lots of mileage clocked up and down our hallway. It was a happy time for all of us as our little family solidified, reaching its zenith in terms of sheer fun and deep connection.

Ryan was growing taller and running faster, now often *beating* the determined Katie in races.

"Yesss! *Victory!*" he'd shout, jumping in the air and high-fiving me as Katie ran around him in circles, breathless in defeat, and ready to try again.

As Ryan matured, he had developed into a rambunctious, athletic eleven-year-old, adept at Little League baseball and utterly consumed with soccer. Proudly outfitted in his uniform—black shorts with an orange T-shirt—he'd run down to Pearl's apartment, raring to go.

"C'mon Graaaaanny!" he implored, stretching out her name just the way I did it. "There's a game at noon—and you've got to come."

Pearl would drop everything, put on a red baseball cap and sunglasses, and hike over to the Battery Park City Ball Field a mile away to watch her boy play. There she was, cheering enthusiastically from the sidelines along with John, me, and Katie—who would try to break free from her red leash.

My frustrated dog would have done anything to get into the action, but, instead, she sat at attention, jealously watching the game. Her wet black nose twitched as she followed the players.

The way she nervously kept looking up at me seemed to say, *"Dad, let me loose! I gotta get out there. The kid needs me,"* which indeed he did.

Afterward, with Ryan still wired up from the game and bursting with energy, he'd slam soccer balls down our 120-foot hallway, showing off his deft footwork as Granny cheered and Katie chased him around, at last relieved to get into the fray.

On weekends, Ryan had friends over from school. No matter how much the boys hooted, hollered, and roughhoused, Katie wasn't fazed in the least by the ruckus. She'd chase those fifth-graders up and down, keeping an ever-watchful eye on Ryan, growling if one of the boys attempted to wrestle him to the ground.

Despite Ryan's ability to shake the house down with his soccer kicks and high spirits, he was also an inquisitive, sensitive boy—chatterbox smart, respectful, and very adult for his years.

Although he wasn't particularly interested in science or math, he liked geography, history, and English—and was all over computers and gadgets.

Blessed with excellent hand-eye coordination, his main interest (continuing to this day) was video games.

He spent hours entertaining himself with his Game Boy, the handheld video game by Nintendo, which he was becoming addicted to. He never left home without the gadget, even when he went down the hall to visit Pearl. This sometimes offended Pearl's sense of decorum.

"Put that thing away until you're done eating!" was Pearl's frequent refrain after Ryan snuck his Game Boy into dinner under his T-shirt, darting repeated glances at it as he ate. Other times, he would switch it off—reluctantly. But he knew his reward would be his favorite chocolate pie, which she only made sometimes as a special treat.

John, of course, was kept apprised of all this, as he frequently conferred with Pearl over that same chocolate pie.

Pearl admired how effectively John managed to balance work with parenting. He was at every teacher-parent conference, helped coach the soccer team, arranged playdates with other parents, and took Ryan to movies, the zoo, you name it.

While John always respected Ryan's privacy and never entered his bedroom without knocking first, this was a nicety Katie never ascribed to. She would barge her way into his bedroom whenever she got the chance, jumping up on him and distracting him from homework.

I loved listening to Ryan tell me all about school, or watching him read a book in my living room with Katie parked next to him, her head on his lap. I always had my camera handy and wound up taking hundreds of pictures. Katie would stare into the camera, poised as always.

One day, I was in my office at my computer, showing Ryan how to type. Katie looked on, sitting next to us on a desk chair, staring at the keys.

Afterward, Ryan got off his chair and Katie jumped up on it. When I came back into the room a few minutes later, there was Katie, pushing her paws up and down on the keys, "typing" away while staring at the monitor and watching the parade of letters, imitating Ryan as she always did.

"Maybe she can write your next book!" giggled Ryan.

Later that day, when Pearl heard about Katie's latest caper, she laughed, "Between changing channels on the TV and typing, maybe you can get her on *Ripley's Believe It or Not*."

It was during these years that John and I became closer to Pearl than ever as we sat around "home base," her dining table, savoring the lively conversation and good food that could always be found in 3C.

Although forty years separated us, "Pa-Re-El" was a complete contemporary. She was up-to-date on tennis, golf, and baseball; current on showbiz gossip and the stock market; avidly listened to radio and TV news; and liked to talk about the wonders of the Internet and the "magic" of faxes.

She was also our resident critic, as good as anyone. "Oprah gets it right every time," she pronounced, "but Geraldo should retire." Although modern in her thinking, she wasn't necessarily interested in adopting technology foreign to her, so she had no cell phone and drew the line on computers as well.

Since John was such a computer whiz, he tried to talk Granny into learning how to use one, but she just waved him away with her hand. "What do I need it for? I keep all my recipes in this index box, and when I want to talk to somebody I use the phone or write a letter." Case closed.

She was, however, much more interested in a before-dinner drink. "I love beer," she told us, swigging one back, "which is why I bought lots of Anheuser-Busch stock. It's always a good bet and I'm never going to lose on it."

"She has opinions on everything," John would tell me, "and you can't stop her from offering them."

"We'd better not try it," I replied.

One interest that brought me closer to Pearl was an activity that I always had enjoyed (and one she fought me on)—planning at-home parties, the more complicated the better.

We'd sit for hours at her dining table, creating the guest lists, menus, and themes. "I think you're crazy going to all this trouble," she'd reply, though she wound up being energized by the prospect of what I had in mind. Secretly, I always thought my party schemes were therapeutic for Pearl, a great way to keep her feeling useful and fully engaged.

One of the most creative was a Halloween dinner for sixteen, complete with towering goblin figures on the table, spooky background music, and scary-looking desserts that tasted better than they looked. Katie came dressed as Cleopatra, with a golden crown on her head and a multicolored doggie caftan.

Ryan loved this party too and raced around the living room in a Batman cape, attempting to scare the crowd while stealing as many orange-frosted cookies as possible. He reveled in all the party action up and down the hall as much as anyone. He may not have had a brother or sister, but he sure had lots of friends of all ages, including many of mine.

One of his favorites was my decorator friend Michael, who had, years before, helped me purchase Baby, the pug that I returned the very next day. Michael had a very wide smile with perfect teeth—and I had always jokingly asked him to "Give me your biggest!"—meaning his exuberant smile.

Ryan caught right onto that, and it became a running joke. When Michael was visiting, he'd playfully goad the little boy, telling him, "Give me *your* biggest"—and Ryan would break out into a huge smile, mimicking Michael, the two of them grinning at each other like chimpanzees.

Maybe you had to be there, but it was pretty funny—and Ryan was always slaphappy to see Michael.

"When's the next party?" Ryan would ask me eagerly, sometimes helping with the name cards or party favors, even when he wasn't invited.

Granny and I brainstormed for days about a surprise birthday party for fourteen magazine editors honoring my longtime friend Susan Ungaro, then the editor in chief of *Family Circle*. The owner chef from a local restaurant came on-site to cook the lunch, and Marie Osmond, whom I had interviewed previously, generously supplied the party favors—hand-painted porcelain dolls. "I think you've completely lost it," Granny surmised, delighted nonetheless by the chocolate-raspberry cake, her idea.

The year's biggest sugar high was Pearl's annual Valentine's Day luncheon, where Katie, dressed in a red hat, sat on a chair at the table with her favorite group of eighty-year-olds. She ate a special heart-shaped dog bone while the others had chocolate hearts, all of us on our way to becoming diabetics.

And each year, I hosted a birthday party for my close friend Bud, debonair and movie-star handsome in his eighties. A Broadway-show fanatic, Bud loved it when Pearl would bring over her vintage collection of Broadway programs, reminiscing about productions dating back to the 1920s and 1930s. (Pearl would shoo Katie away when she tried to "peruse" one with her teeth.)

"It was great meeting someone even older than me who could present something from the past," Bud reflected, "and we always played a little quiz about our favorite shows."

Pearl had seen nearly every production on the Great White Way, as had Bud. "But my favorite," she smiled dreamily, showing Bud the original program, "was *The King and I* because I loved Yul Brynner. *There* was a man."

Most of the time Pearl was in a festive mood, and she'd

come and stay for the entire party, enjoying it from beginning to end. At other times, she'd make a grand entrance just at dessert time.

Like Ed McMahon introducing Johnny Carson, I'd announce: "Heeeeeeeeeeeere's Granny!" and into the room she'd burst, Katie at her side, beaming as everyone applauded.

"I have the cutest date in the room," Pearl once laughed, pointing at Katie as she sat down, plunking my dog on her lap as she took all of my guests in with a discerning, somewhat sardonic look.

In October 1997, I planned an eighty-fifth birthday party for Granny, a lunch for thirty, complete with helium balloons, flowers, place cards, a rented thirty-foot table with ballroom chairs, and a chocolate cake made by one of my favorite bakeries, the Cupcake Café, which specialized in intricately true-to-life buttercream flowers.

"Please don't bother," said Granny, resisting such an elaborate party, and disapproving of all the expense. Pearl was the kind of woman who always took a bus, rarely a taxi, who kept a refrigerator filled with leftovers, and who ate out only occasionally, mostly when she was in the mood for the incomparable pastrami at the Second Avenue Deli in the East Village. Otherwise, she was a homebody.

"Anita, I've tried and tried to tell Glenn not to be so extravagant, but it only makes him mad," she told my mom, who had become close friends with Pearl.

"Well," Mom said, "you can forget about changing him. Even as a kid, he was setting the table for my parties—so just let him do it."

And she did. On the day of the party, we got Katie all dressed up, just as she always was for every party.

"Which one should it be?" I asked Granny. We had two

glitzy doggie dresses to choose from, both gifts from Katie's modeling jobs. There was either a multicolored sequined dress with a yellow satin collar or a black satin taffeta getup with ruffled fabric at the tail, complete with purple and yellow flowers embroidered all over it.

"They're both pretty gaudy," Granny laughed, "but the taffeta — good for afternoon."

Katie understood that a party was in the works and had no problem donning the costume, expertly so, daintily stepping into it by pushing her paws through the arm holes, then staying still while I attached the Velcro in the back.

Then off she flew down the hall to promenade around the living room of my apartment, racing to the window, twirling in circles, then jumping up on the green-and-beige lounge chair to peruse her kingdom from above. She posed for pictures with Pearl until she got bored, then hung her head over the thick cushion, staring down at the floor as she scratched her ears.

"My little baby looks so pretty!" exclaimed Granny, attractively outfitted that day in blue linen.

And so it was that Granny and Katie were our family's "party girls," expert hostesses whose social season peaked with this special birthday party, an affair to remember.

Overexcited, Katie jumped down from the chair in my bedroom, and her tail hilariously stuck out from the black satin ruffles as she skipped back down the hallway to Pearl's apartment. Ryan and John came by to pick up Katie and Pearl — and Katie raced back down to my apartment with her favorites following from behind. It was a whirl of activity.

That day, Pearl held court amid the ivory and gold balloons, birthday hats, noisemakers, and elephant-and-tiger printed napkins. And despite herself, she was delighted by all the attention.

When the twelve-inch chocolate cake came out, Ryan and a few neighborhood girls quickly surrounded Granny and helped her blow out her candles. Katie pushed her way into the picture as well.

Pearl hugged Ryan tightly, "You're my boy!"

"Happy birthday, *Oldest*!"

Pearl's final words to me?

"I've never had a birthday party. *Don't* do it again!"

CHAPTER SIXTEEN

The Talking Picture Frame

I n the late 1990s, after five years of support groups, therapy, and physical rehabilitation, my back (and the depression) had finally healed completely and I was able to return to writing. Instead of a grueling high-pressure newspaper job with tight deadlines and constant travel, however, I switched gears entirely, working from home as a freelance contributor to *Family Circle*.

It was a perfect fit. Gone were the tabloid stories, the celebrity column, and the movie star interviews. Instead, I now concentrated on what were new niches for me — self-help, inspiration, and service-related articles, all in keeping with my priorities in life — family, friends, and dogs (and not always in that order).

I researched and wrote about whatever intrigued me. Some of my favorite articles included "The Best Decision I Ever Made," "Are You Looking for the Good Life or the Good *in* Life?" "Should Your Child Watch TV News?" "How to Be a People Magnet," "Create the Life You Want," "The Positive Power of Friendship," "Putting Gratitude in Your Attitude," "Why Laughter Is Good for You," and my all-time favorite — "The

Secrets of the Centenarians." I was fascinated by the phenom-
enon of longevity.

Reading about a 107-year-old woman in my story, Granny
was puzzled. "Why," she asked me, "did she make a decision to
get *remarried* at *ninety-nine*?"

I told her what the woman had told me, "Just optimistic, I
guess!"

"But her new husband was twenty years younger," Granny
exclaimed, titillated by this golden years romance that included
drinking Champagne, dancing, and acting together in theatrical productions.

I picked up the magazine and read to Granny the woman's reason for dating a younger man, "I robbed the cradle! He
was lonesome. I wasn't, but I enjoyed his company so we fell in
love."

Granny, who had no interest in a new suitor, was nonetheless intrigued by this subject. One of the greatest secrets of longevity, aside from genetics, is the ability to shake off stress and
stay involved in life, just as Granny had by getting so intimately
involved with Katie, John, Ryan, and me. The "centenarian
personality," I had learned, is a mind-set that combines positive
thinking and a fighting spirit. That was Granny.

And so, it was during this time that I made up my mind to
write an entire article about my relationship with Pearl, and I
titled it "Granny Down the Hall: From Friendship to Family."
It was the first and only time, until now, that I'd ever written
about my life and the people in it.

The opening lines of the story said it all, *"Some of the
best things that happen in life are purely accidental. A friendship
sometimes develops when you least expect it. That's what happened
to me."*

Here was our story, all about the coincidence of living in

the same hallway, about how our little family had been accidentally created and cemented together by my precocious puppy.

Whether it was serendipity, luck, chemistry, or sheer proximity, my first brief encounter with Pearl and the events that followed it had changed my life (and my dog's) forever.

Writing the article was bittersweet, as the key person who had first introduced me to Pearl was no longer there to read it. Joe, my good friend and dog mentor, had died a year earlier of AIDS. He'd been incredibly brave, fighting to the end by keeping himself active, always looking forward to life—investing in real estate, picking up gardening as a hobby, and getting two new dogs (collies this time) after Dinah died. I would never forget his wisdom and kindness a decade earlier, when he encouraged me to get a dog and taught me how to train one. We all missed him—as he was certainly part of our story.

During the photo shoot for the article (Pearl's first), we posed at her dining room table. One of Ryan's arms was around my neck, his other around Pearl's shoulder, with Katie wedged between us. You couldn't take a bad picture of Ryan, who was now a lanky and very handsome eleven-year-old, happy-go-lucky and intrigued by all the attention being paid to him.

Although Pearl, Ryan, and John were a little shy about having a magazine photograph taken, Katie sure wasn't. Now nearly twelve, she was just about as energetic as always. An experienced model, she pushed herself into the center of every frame and stared at the camera, never blinking at the flashes. Betty had groomed her to within an inch of her life, and her blond hair was shining that day, her ears never fluffier. She was an old pro and a big ham.

Even when the photographer wanted to snap just Pearl and Ryan cooking together at the stove, Katie objected. She pushed against the photographer's legs repeatedly until he boosted her up on the kitchen counter and submitted to her desire to stay front and center. In the shot, her nose poked down into the frying pan as Pearl stirred the eggs.

When the article was published, something about it seemed to really touch readers because it turned out to be one of the most popular pieces I'd ever written.

Despite Pearl's innate modesty and her initial disinterest in being in the limelight, she was nonetheless excited about *this*! After I gave her copies of the article with the full-color photos, she started handing them out to all her friends in our building.

For most of her life, Pearl had lived in the background — modestly leading what some might call a fairly ordinary existence, certainly never seeking the limelight in any public way. With her huge heart and able hands, she'd always been helping *others*, most notably her husband and her family, and, of course, us.

But now — she was the STAR!

It was on the crest of this success, with our family at its closest, that some profound events occurred that would soon change it all.

John had been actively looking for a mate and finally met someone whom he was becoming quite serious about. While Granny had given the thumbs-down on many of John's dates (typically saying, "Oh, my goodness, that guy, forget him"), John's new beau, Peter, was a warmhearted person who appealed to Pearl. A successful corporate headhunter, Peter was a nurturing kind of person with a gift for turning a house into a home.

While down-to-earth, practical John was possibly the most nonmaterialistic person I knew — paying little attention to clothing, furniture, or anything remotely connected to what he considered "luxury"—Peter was just the opposite. He was an avid collector of furniture, art, and jewelry. And his large apartment near Carnegie Hall was filled with stylish accents and effects completely foreign to Midwestern John.

They were such opposites. Peter was compulsively neat, driven, and superorganized, while John was more relaxed and casual, but it was a good balance. Each had what the other needed. John wanted a stable partner and a comfortable home, while Peter, with such a beautiful home and nobody in it, wanted a family.

Watching them together, I could see how much John enjoyed Peter's take-charge attitude and easy affection; and Peter was touched by John's devotion to Ryan and by the way John had succeeded in balancing his responsibilities.

I admit that having Peter on the scene made me uncomfortable and, at times, resentful, because his presence shifted the balance of attention—leaving Granny and me somewhat left behind.

It wasn't long before Peter was spending more and more time on our floor. He upgraded John's sparsely appointed apartment into a homier nest, bringing in curtains, rugs, lamps, and plants while also filling out both John's and Ryan's wardrobe. John was happy and excited with the turn of events, while Pearl welcomed Peter into her dining room, making him a part of our group.

The downside for us was that, in May 2000, exactly seven years after John and Ryan had moved in, John announced that he was moving uptown, into Peter's more spacious apartment. Happy as I was for him, I was disappointed too, not wanting to lose them.

"It's time for us to leave," John told me quietly. "We're going to miss you and Granny a lot! But this is a big step forward for me, and I'm moving for a happy reason," though it wasn't happy for everyone.

"I'm so sad," I confided to Pearl one day. "I'm going to miss them so much. Do you think John's doing the right thing?"

"You never know until you try—but he's wanted this for a long time, so we have to let him go," she wisely answered.

"But Ryan—what are we going to do without him?" I asked. She had no answer to that one. The hallway was going to be empty without him, and Katie wasn't going to like it either.

I loved that kid—having him over as he did his homework, watching TV with him, laughing about anything and everything, taking him places with Katie, going out for holidays— all the things we'd done together for years. I couldn't imagine life without either him or John. Neither could Granny—so we both dreaded the inevitable.

On the final moving day, Ryan came into Pearl's apartment to say good-bye to us. "I'm going to visit you all the time," he told Granny, giving her a huge hug and kiss.

"You'd better!" said Granny, handing John a tinfoil-covered plate of cookies for the road.

Katie jumped on Ryan's lap. As if somehow understanding what was happening, she put her paws around him and licked his face over and over again.

"Good-bye, girlie," Ryan whispered. "I'll come back to see you."

And then, Ryan handed Pearl two going-away presents. The first was a small pink rhododendron that Ryan had taken good care of, watering it as Pearl had instructed him to. (Thereafter, it became Pearl's favorite plant.)

Next, he handed her a small package wrapped in tissue paper, which would become one of her most treasured possessions.

She opened it up, and there was a framed photograph of Granny and Ryan, one of the pictures taken for the magazine article.

"And look," said Ryan, turning the frame over for Granny. "The best part is that it's a *talking* picture frame!"

"A what?" asked Granny, puzzled by this.

"Look here, when you press this button, you hear a recording that I made—just for you, Oldest."

Pearl then pressed the button, and out came a message: "*Hi Granny, it's Ryan. Love you. You too, Katie. Don't ever forget me.*" Then there was the sound of a kiss. "Love, Ryan."

"Grannsy," John said in parting, hugging Pearl close, "we're gonna come down next week for some of that chocolate pie!"

"That's a date," she answered.

She opened her front door and sadly watched Ryan and John walk down the long hallway to the elevator, waving good-bye.

And then...they were gone.

How could things ever be the same again?

CHAPTER SEVENTEEN

Lady Sings the Blues

After John and Ryan moved out, our red-carpeted hallway became eerily quiet. After seven happy years, all the action and excitement ground to a halt.

Pearl's daily trips to the school bus and the babysitting were over. Gone were the card games and hours spent laughing at her dining table. Ryan now had an "official" nanny of his own, a second dad too, and even two dogs, a surly Lhasa apso named Virgil and a hyperkinetic papillon named Chance. All of them displaced the family he'd known, including my lonesome dog.

At first, poor Katie scouted down the hallway every day. She scratched at Ryan's door and lay next to it, sadly waiting for her young friend to return. She was despondent without him.

"Oh, Katie girl," I whispered, picking her up in my arms and taking her back down to Pearl's. "Ryan isn't here anymore, but he still loves you."

"*But Dad,*" she seemed to say, pulling against me and returning to his door, "*I gotta wait for him. I miss him.*"

"I know you do, sweetheart. I do too. But he's gone."

But the very next day, Katie would run right back down the

hall to Ryan's door and poke her nose into it, desperately trying to find him.

Pearl wasn't any happier than Katie. Although my dog and I showed up at her door just as much as ever, things seemed very different. After all, Ryan wasn't racing in and out with Katie at his heel; John was no longer asking Pearl for advice about his dates or planning outings. And our family dinners were no more.

Sure, John and Ryan periodically phoned Oldest and me or came over to visit. We shared desserts at Pearl's dining table, but it just wasn't the same as their living down the hall. I missed taking care of "the kid," and hearing him tell me all about school. I also felt sadly numb without John—I had lost my favorite confidante and on-site friend. But John was busy adjusting to his new relationship and environs while Ryan was getting used to a different school and new friends; they were both understandably busy with their new lives. And so I worried for Granny.

Everybody in life needs a support system—whether it's family or friends or a surrogate family like the one we had created. Pearl had definitely lost a big part of the support she had grown to depend on, especially after Arthur's death.

As John later reflected, "It was sad because Ryan didn't get as much time to spend with Grannsy—though we did visit as much as we could—but I think she took it [the separation] harder than we did."

Indeed, although Pearl typically kept her feelings private, around this time she began pouring her heart out to her longtime friend Rose, a vivacious, glamorous woman who had worked in the fashion industry with the French designer Givenchy. (Rose's husband, Alvin, and Arthur had been business associates.) She was also a highly skilled astrologer, extraordinarily sensitive about people, and sought after by a number of celebrity clients.

Rose, who lived across the river from us in Fort Lee, New Jersey, could easily see the dramatic transformation in Pearl's spirits as our family had evolved.

"Having Ryan in her life gave her purpose, something to look forward to every day," recalled Rose. "But when Ryan moved away, she was heartbroken. She was calling me every day, crying on the phone. She felt terribly lonesome."

"Listen, Pearl," Rose told her. "Nothing in life lasts forever. People come into our lives for a reason when we need them— and everybody moves on."

"I know it. I know."

"I'll mention something to Glenn. Maybe he can do something about it."

"No," Pearl answered quickly.

"Don't take it so personally," Rose continued. "Even if you were his real grandmother, you probably wouldn't see him as much as you were used to. After all, Ryan is growing up and kids his age want to be with their friends. That's just the way it is."

But as Rose later reflected, "It was hard for Pearl to accept. She felt she was no longer needed. She told me it was like losing Arthur all over again."

⌘

At the grand age of eighty-eight, with her "boy" gone, it was as if someone had put a pin in the balloon of Pearl's spirits. She was still relatively robust, far ahead of most of her contemporaries, and continued to do all her own shopping and cooking. But as I watched her do it all, I could tell she was just going through the motions. Her desire to cook and bake had slowed way down, just as her pleasure in life was flagging. She was definitely depressed.

Some days, as I passed her door, I heard music coming through it, and more often than not she was playing one of her favorite Billie Holiday LPs featuring "Lady Sings the Blues," one of the signature songs written by the jazz singer. The mournful music was somehow in tune with the mood of our hallway without Ryan.

Things were now falling through the cracks. Although Pearl had never been a fastidious housekeeper, her apartment was more disheveled than usual. Half the time, she didn't make her bed, while Arthur's single bed was always perfectly made and empty, a reminder of her loss. More and more, she looked through a huge, messy drawer of old photos, lost in the memories of her past life. All this made me terribly sad. I tried to keep up her spirits by inviting her *out* to dinner, though she often declined.

Most distressing to me, Pearl's always sharp mind was now a bit vague. Some days, she seemed disoriented and distracted. I'd find her wandering around outside near our local drugstore, window-shopping, with a blank look on her face. But she snapped right back to her old self once we started talking, forcing her to focus.

"How's my sweet little girlie?" she cooed at Katie, who jumped right up on her Granny, as always.

"Ouch! Those nails are sharp. When are you going to see Betty?"

While previously always in command of Katie while walking her, Pearl was now almost pulled off-balance when Katie pulled back on the leash, as she was often prone to do.

After a general checkup, we learned that Oldest had high blood pressure and that she was also anemic, which explained why she seemed dizzy at times, often wobbly on her feet. Her overall energy level was faltering.

Although never one to speak about her health, Pearl now complained about cramps, stomach pains, and problems with digestion. She delayed going to a specialist, though I pushed her to do it. Right into the summer of 2001, I continued lecturing her about having an exam. "You've got to take care of yourself and get that colonoscopy."

"Stop it!" she snapped. "I'll do it when I'm ready. Stop worrying. I'm fine." But she really wasn't, which is why I found it difficult to stop myself from nagging her.

Meanwhile, Katie was now a dowager with various ailments of her own, mostly arthritis and failing vision. At age thirteen, although she was still happy to walk outside and game to chase her blue rubber ball up and down the hall, she couldn't run as fast or as long as before, and she sometimes bumped into the wall.

"Katie has cataracts," Dr. Simon told me, "though she's still seeing most of what she needs to. Eventually we can consider removing them, but for now, let's leave her alone."

We had always walked the three flights of cement stairs up from and down to the lobby of our building. But Katie slipped one day, falling down the stairs and landing on her side. She let out a screech and was crying in pain—and confusion. I scooped her up in my arms to soothe her, feeling terrible about it, and took her to the vet for an X-ray. "Katie," Dr. Simon told me, "was very lucky. Nothing broken or bruised—just her ego."

But after that, we always took the elevator, as Katie no longer had the strength in her legs, or the balance, to negotiate the steps.

Likewise, although my dog tried to jump on my bed as she always had when she was ready for a nap or bedtime, she could no longer make it. One day I saw her try to make the jump, but she fell backward onto the carpet—looking bewildered and indignant. After that, I purchased a little carpeted staircase of three steps that allowed her to walk up on the bed. That problem was solved.

"My little girl is getting to be a senior!" cooed Pearl, still avidly interested in every aspect of Katie's care and condition. Although she walked Katie less than she used to, she babysat her just as much as ever. But more and more of their time was spent together in bed taking long naps, often with the TV blaring.

It was discouraging seeing them slowed down, frail, and, at times, so apathetic. And yet it was also incredibly sweet watching these two soulmates snuggle together, each giving the other the comfort and tenderness they needed.

As for me, with Ryan and John gone, and Granny and Katie ailing, I wasn't very happy, feeling that life in Battery Park City was no longer the fun-filled place it once had been. I had no idea, however, how dramatically our lives were about to change.

CHAPTER EIGHTEEN

The Day Our World Stopped

Tuesday, September 11, 2001, was a picture perfect day in New York City, sunny and warm. After an early-morning jog, I sat at my computer typing letters, while Katie was lying under my desk, her head resting on my right foot, lazily content.

The view outside my window to the coast of New Jersey was dazzling that morning. The mirrored wall in my home office reflected the clear blue skies and the Hudson River, smooth as glass with its commuter boats, small yachts, and sailboats. All of it was framed by a lush row of trees so close to my windows that my office looked a little like an enchanted forest.

But the calm was shattered at 8:46 a.m. by a strange-sounding explosive boom that echoed through my apartment. The entire building seemed to vibrate. At first, though, I ignored it.

Since there were always construction projects going on in the neighborhood, I assumed the noise was just routine, though it was louder than anything I'd ever heard before.

Puzzled, I looked out at the river but saw nothing and returned to work.

Then the phone rang.

"Turn on the TV!" ordered Pearl, her voice uncharacteristically agitated. "An airplane just crashed into the World Trade Center. Watch it." And she hung up the phone.

I switched on the small TV in my office and was startled to see the North Tower of the Trade Center *on fire*.

I rushed into the living room, where I had a full view of the Twin Towers.

The crash and the small blaze seemed so peculiar. How could what emerging TV reports were describing as a "small commuter plane" accidentally fly into such a mammoth building?

As smoke and flames poured out of the building, I had the surreal experience of watching this event unfold on TV while simultaneously seeing it, directly from my windows.

Had it been Monday instead of Tuesday, I would have been in the Trade Center myself, on the way from the subway station there to my volunteer job as a hotline counselor. I was in and out of the Towers daily; in addition to the subway, I was always in the shopping arcade, frequenting the drugstore, newsstand, bakery, clothing stores, hotel, and bank.

A number of my neighbors worked in the Towers, and many of them were there on this day.

And now, as we would later learn, a team of al-Qaeda suicide hijackers had crashed American Airlines Flight 11 into the North Tower, instantly killing as many as 600 people.

At first, it seemed as if the disaster was under control.

But seventeen minutes later, of course, a second team of hijackers crashed United Airlines Flight 175 into the South Tower.

Immediately after seeing *that* on TV and knowing that ours was the closest residential building to the Towers, perhaps next in line, I had to do something.

My heart was racing as I heard the high-pitched sound of police and fire truck sirens, getting louder and louder as they all converged in the streets. I tucked Katie into my bedroom, snatched up my keys and wallet, and ran down the stairs to the lobby.

It was pandemonium.

Panicked tenants rushed out the front circular door, half-dressed, some fearfully asking questions, others in tears.

Through the floor-to-ceiling glass windows of the lobby, I could see people shouting and running wild—jumping over the hedges and racing toward the Hudson.

Terrified mothers pushing baby carriages were everywhere, uncertain about what to do next.

Firefighters swarmed around the complex, overwhelmed and confused themselves.

Residents were practically assaulting our petrified door-man, Felipe, asking about evacuation plans for the building.

"You've got to get out!" was his brisk command. "Evacuate. Walk south."

A woman I'd never seen before (or since) was lying on the lobby floor next to the couch, her face covered in blood. I dashed back upstairs to grab some paper towels, Band-Aids, and bottled water, but when I got back downstairs, the woman was gone.

I ran back up the stairs again and knocked on Pearl's door. She opened it looking shaken, very pale, and somewhat in shock.

"We've got to go now," she said, locking up her door and leaving her apartment without her purse, just her house keys clutched in her hand. She wasn't dressed warmly enough, in a sleeveless, salmon-colored blouse and gray tweed skirt, but she probably figured she'd be returning home soon.

"Granny," I said, "you go downstairs and wait for me by the front desk. I'll be right down. I just have to get Katie and my cell phone. Wait for me!"

"All right," she answered absently, "but hurry."

As she walked down the hall to the elevator, she looked so frail, and yet so brave. My heart broke at just the sight of her. Here she was, nearly ninety, not in the greatest of spirits or health and having to face something like this.

When I got back inside my apartment, I turned off the lights and TV and put a few blank checks in my wallet. I scooped Katie up, frantically hitching her to her red leash, and then rushed to the elevator. Having already been out for a walk just a few hours earlier, she dragged behind me, resistant to my disrupting her nap schedule.

When I got down to the front desk, Granny was gone.

"Felipe," I asked nervously, "where's Pearl?" And he pointed out toward the back door, just behind his desk. "She just walked away," he said, accosted on all sides by other tenants.

Why in the world would Granny leave without me? I rushed out back behind our building, and carefully surveyed the walkway in both directions, searching furiously, but Pearl was gone.

As we headed south on the Esplanade, Katie was a stalwart little soldier. She walked obediently beside me, though she was clearly petrified by the loud noises and wild stampede of people swarming around us. She had always hated loud sounds—and this was the worst. But with an anxious look in her eye, her head swinging from side to side, she plowed on, limping slightly due to arthritis.

"*Dad, I'm afraid!*" she seemed to tell me with those worried brown eyes. "*Please, I can't walk. Let's go home.*"

"Katie, no, no, we can't go back. Come on, you can do it. Let's go!"

After a few more minutes, I stopped and just picked Katie up in my arms, staring up at the burning Towers, watching those poor souls trapped inside, many of them huddled at the windows, gasping for air.

I noticed a young child nearby, naively looking up at this burning inferno and remarking to his mom, "Look, Mommy, *birds*!" His mom shielded his eyes, for those "birds" were actually people jumping out of the smoke-filled windows.

Horrified, I turned away.

And then, just a few moments later, at 9:59 a.m., as we continued trudging south, I felt a ferocious vibration, a horrible kind of ominous rumble. The South Tower had collapsed, toppling to the ground like an accordion, though I had no idea what was happening at the time.

We were suddenly in a total blackout—with thick black dust and debris raining down on us. I would later read that 2,000 tons of asbestos and 424,000 tons of concrete were used to build the Twin Towers, and half of it now came crashing down, the air laden with toxins.

The formerly sunny sky was instantly blackened by this thunderstorm of suffocating soot and ash. You could feel the heat of the explosion on your face. I was coughing and couldn't see anything in front of me.

Standing there in silence, surrounded by hundreds of others, I had no idea what to do next. I bent down to check on Katie and panicked when I saw that she had fallen over and was choking, unable to breathe.

I frantically brushed away the black soot from her face and

picked her up in my arms, shouting to a firefighter coming toward us. I pulled him by his arm as he tried to rush by me. "Please, please, stop! I need your help. My dog isn't breathing."

His face was dripping with sweat as he bent down and took a quick look at Katie. "Her nose is packed with soot," he said—and then blasted water into her nose using a pressurized water bottle he had in his hand, telling me it would force her to expel the dust. And it worked! She immediately sprang to life again, stood up, and climbed into my arms.

"Thank you!" I told him, incredibly grateful and relieved, but he was already gone.

At this moment, in the midst of the utter chaos and confusion, I oddly enough felt taken care of, even comforted, for nothing but kindness prevailed.

People held hands and offered bottles of water, tissues, and wet towels. I saw younger people holding onto the arms of seniors, guiding them patiently away from the explosion. Without any pushing, neighbors young and old, with babies and dogs, trooped south, where police boats were waiting to evacuate everyone to New Jersey.

Firefighters passed around dust masks for the elderly and children, but there weren't enough for everyone. An older woman next to me was coughing badly, so I took off my shirt, poured water over it, and gave it to her. "Cover your face and breathe through it," I told her, relieved to be cool in just a T-shirt.

And then, at 10:28 a.m., another implosion began, the same horrible noise as before, as astonishingly, the North Tower collapsed.

"Down, down, down!" shouted a nearby policeman, screeching at the top of his lungs. "Get on the ground, now, everybody, stomach down!" And we threw ourselves onto the pavement, covering our heads, buried in dust. Katie was under my chest, protected, breathing heavily as she cowered beneath me, now shivering. "Shhhhh, Shhhhh," I told her, holding her in place. "It's okay."

But it wasn't okay at all. The world was collapsing around us, crushing our beautiful neighborhood, killing our residents, and forever changing our lives—and the world.

CHAPTER NINETEEN

The Escape

A few minutes later, I got up off the ground and brushed myself off. Most of the people around me had blackened faces and everybody looked stunned, or worse. Now my only thought was of Granny.

Where *was* she? It would be futile trying to find her in this cloud of black dust, but I dreaded the thought of her being trapped in the dark, alone and afraid.

As I would later find out, after Pearl wandered off down the walkway, she was approached by an incredibly kind, very pretty woman named Lee—a financial planner in her fifties who lived in our building. Blond-haired with brilliant blue eyes and a warm sisterly air, Lee had a large retinue of elderly women friends that she watched over. She recognized Pearl, but they had never met.

"Pearl," Lee remembers, "was standing in the middle of an open area walking around in a circle, dazed, looking up at the Towers."

"Would you like to come sit with us?" Lee asked, hospitably pointing to a bench of her women friends.

"Sure, thanks," answered Pearl, shivering in the breeze

despite the warmth of the day. She was grateful that one of the women offered her a black cardigan.

Soon, with hundreds of people running south on the Esplanade, the police instructed the women around Pearl and Lee to likewise begin moving the quarter-mile distance toward the southern tip of the Battery where police boats were waiting. But, exhausted and frightened, Pearl had no desire to go anywhere, as she was searching furiously for me and Katie.

"Please," she told Lee. "Just leave me here and go ahead. I can't go. I'm waiting for someone."

But Lee gently persuaded Pearl to get up and start walking, "slowly, very slowly," said Lee, "because I could see that Pearl wasn't very strong."

When the first Tower fell, Pearl cried out, gripping Lee's arm in panic, choking on the dust. "Just close your eyes and breathe through this," said Lee calmly, putting a stray jacket she'd found over Pearl's head. She then led Pearl half-blindly to the railing by the water to steady her.

"Down, down, down!" shouted the police, ordering everyone to lie next to a stone wall flat on their stomachs with their hands over their heads. There could be another attack, another nearby building might fall, or there could be a gas explosion.

Getting down on the ground was impossible for Pearl and she refused to do it. But she hadn't counted on the persistent Lee, who enlisted the help of a young man. He gladly lifted Pearl in his arms and gently placed her down next to Lee.

So there they were, these brand-new friends, huddled on the cement together. "Her frail little hands were ice-cold the entire time," recalled Lee, "and she never loosened her grip on her house keys, clenching them in her right hand while she held my hand with her left. I kept talking to keep her busy."

And then the second Tower collapsed. "It felt like an

earthquake and I just hugged Pearl close, keeping my arms around her. To keep her distracted, I asked, 'Pearl, what's your middle name?' "

And that's when Granny's inimitable wit returned. "I don't have one. I guess we were too poor to get one!" And Pearl broke into a laugh. For months after that, Lee and Pearl would always joke about this moment.

A few minutes later, Lee and Pearl were up again, walking slowly through the mayhem toward the South Cove marina, where police boats were waiting. Although it was ordinarily a short five-minute walk away, the distance seemed much greater to Granny, who had no inclination to continue.

"Pearl kept telling me to leave her," said Lee, "that she was an old woman and was going to die anyway, but I just ignored that and got some water, splashing it in her face."

Lee noticed an injured fireman being loaded onto a police boat headed toward Jersey City, and overheard someone saying that there was room for just a few more civilians. The motorboat was already packed to its capacity with twenty-five passengers. "Listen," she told the captain, "there's an eighty-nine-year-old woman with me, and if you don't get her on this boat, she's not going to make it."

"Okay, get her, and we'll take her."

Lee had two young men nearby hoist Pearl onto the boat, literally lifting her off the ground in an instant.

"Leave me alone!" Pearl hollered, nearly hysterical. "I'm not going." But Lee persisted, and watched Pearl being lifted up over the rail.

"Pearl," Lee shouted, "I'll get the next boat and find you over there," but Pearl continued screaming, refusing to be separated from her new friend.

"Take me off!" she commanded, her former strength

suddenly in evidence. "If she's not coming, neither am I! I can't make it without her. *Take me off*!"

Even the police were impressed with this gutsy woman who wasn't going anywhere, terrorists or no terrorists.

The boat waited, everybody made a little extra room, and Lee was ushered aboard. And this group of strangers, huddled together, sped off toward the safety of the Jersey shore, the bumpy water jostling Pearl around as Lee held onto her with both hands.

"Lee," Pearl whispered, completely out of breath, "I need to find my friend Glenn."

⌷⌷

Meanwhile, I resisted the prospect of evacuating Battery Park City until the last possible moment, holding out hope that we might somehow be able to return home.

Katie and I sat on the grass in front of the Museum of Jewish Heritage, a starkly modern glass-and-granite structure located about a half mile from our building. From this perch, I watched the stream of people boarding the boats and moving away toward the opposite shore, scouting for Pearl but never seeing her.

As I sat there, I stroked Katie's stomach absently.

"You've *got* to get on one of those boats," a policeman ordered, not for the first time.

I finally surrendered and moved forward toward the river's edge, approaching the police speedboat that was bobbing unsteadily in the water. I handed Katie over to a passenger already on board, and then jumped on myself. Katie's ears were flying in the wind and her face was smudged and blackened. I held her in my arms as we pulled away, leaving the ravaged Manhattan skyline behind.

When we got to the Jersey side of the Hudson River, I searched, yet again, for Pearl, asking everyone I recognized from our building if they had seen her. But nobody had. Katie was desperately thirsty and a Red Cross volunteer gave me a styrofoam cup filled with water. She greedily gulped it down.

Determined to find a hotel, I began walking west toward the Doubletree Suites, which was about a mile away. Katie was limping badly, but we had to forge ahead. Although I was hoping to get a room for the night, that was impossible. Hundreds of displaced residents were already camped out in the hotel lobby when we got there.

With nowhere to sleep that night and no clothes (much less any dog food or supplies), I called my close friend and longtime editor, Ed, naively hoping he might be able to drive into Jersey and pick us up. Of course, with all the Manhattan tunnels and bridges closed down, this rescue plan was impossible.

"But I have some very close friends who live close by," Ed told me. "Let me call them and see if they'll put you and Katie up for the night."

And within minutes, Ed called me back with the good news. So Katie and I were on the move again, walking a half a mile to a safe retreat.

If there's any redeeming value in disaster, it's seeing what happens when people bond together—offering help, sharing resources, and making new friends. I was touched when Ed's friends, Barbara and Charlie (he had narrowly escaped himself a few hours earlier that day from the North Tower), greeted us at their door with open arms. Their two Labs, Spice and Dune, lumbering on their heels, were curious about me and the new blond-haired intruder.

Katie was exhausted and disoriented. She took a quick sniff at the huge dogs and then walked right past them, her nose drawing her toward the kitchen, where she stole food from their bowls.

"Katie!" I scolded, "that's bad manners." But all was well. Spice and Dune were more interested in snooping at Katie's posterior than protecting their food. And although these two large dogs dwarfed her, she was, as usual, unfazed. Soon, she was lying in a heap on the wooden floor, sound asleep. I slipped out to a nearby store to buy a toothbrush and some other necessities.

That night, as I huddled with my new friends around the TV watching endless replays of the horrendous news of the day, I felt grateful to be alive, thankful to have a place to sleep.

Twelve hours earlier, all had been well in Battery Park City. It had started out as a beautiful summer day. And now, the sun was setting on a neighborhood that would never be the same, the comfort of home gone.

Just before going to sleep, I called John on my cell phone.

"I lost Granny," I told him worriedly, explaining how she had disappeared, "and I don't know what to do."

"We'll figure it out," he told me with certainty, steady as always.

"Just take the ferry back to Manhattan tomorrow, and Ryan and I will pick you up. You and Katie can stay with us. It will be just like old days—we'll be together again!"

For the first time that entire, dreadful day, I was crying. I guess it was John's familiar voice and that down-to-earth logic that got to me.

That night, as I fell into a sound sleep with Katie pressed up against me, I felt so much better, knowing that I was going home again.

⌦

The next day, John and Ryan were waiting at the dock on the Manhattan side of the Hudson as Katie and I got off the ferry boat at Pier 79 near West 39th Street.

"Katie girl!" Ryan shouted, bending down, "COME!"

Katie gleefully bounded into his arms, covering his face with wet kisses.

"Whoa, whoa, girl," he giggled. He took her red leash out of my hand and led her into a taxi, with John and me following.

We headed up to John's new seven-room apartment on West 57th Street, a sprawling well-decorated home far more glamorous than his previous place in our building.

The question on all of our minds was: Where was *Granny*? It was all I could think about. Although Pearl had often talked about her New Jersey relatives, I was drawing a complete blank on their names and had never had their phone number. For the next three days, John and I were stumped. But at last, it was John who pulled from his memory the name. "I did a computer search for Pearl's nephew. It's a very common last name, but I started calling around, and I've found him!"

I practically grabbed that number out of his hand and immediately called. "Granny! Is that *you*?!"

"It's Granny all right—thank God it's *you*," sighed Pearl, who sounded exhausted. She explained that Lee and others from our neighborhood had stayed with her for hours that day until they finally parted that evening. Lee went home with her daughter and left Pearl in the very capable hands of a married couple who lived in our building. They had kindly taken Pearl that first night to stay with *their* relatives in New Jersey. The following night Pearl was driven by them to her own relative's house in nearby Montclair, though she wasn't very happy about it.

"I tried to find you, Glenn...but everything went wrong," she said sadly, her voice trailing off. "Are you okay? What happened to you? How's my girl?" I filled Pearl in on everything and told her how sorry I was that I had lost her.

"And Katie misses you! We're temporarily living with John

and Peter, but I'll call you every day and we'll figure out what to do next."

It became quickly clear that it was going to be impossible to return home anytime soon. There was no electricity, gas, water, or telephone service. Moreover, Battery Park City was now an armed camp, surrounded by the National Guard, the FBI, FEMA's (Federal Emergency Management Agency) Urban Search and Rescue, and the New York City Police Department—the entire neighborhood declared a crime scene.

And just across the street from our complex, the smoldering ruins of the Trade Center site were guarded by the military and overrun by rescue workers who had the grim task of sifting through the debris, removing victims' remains.

In conversations with Pearl over the next day or so, she sounded weak. She said she was fighting a stomach bug, so she insisted that we wait to visit her until she'd had a chance to recuperate.

"Do you have everything you need, Oldest?" I asked her.

"Everything but Katie. Give her a kiss."

Over the next week, as we watched the round-the-clock TV coverage of 9/11, Katie and I settled in with John, Ryan, Peter, and their two dogs—Virgil and Chance.

Middle-aged Virgil was the grouchy alpha dog of the house, snarly and prone to biting anyone in his territory. He instantly disliked Katie (and the feeling was mutual), so Katie was kept gated in the bathroom for her own protection. She moped there on the cold tile floor, barely eating her food, only content when I took her out for walks or when she slept with me at night in the apartment's small office.

John's other dog, Chance, the papillon, was a yappy white ball of fur who irritated Katie, so she simply ignored him, or slapped him away with her paw.

Aside from the stress of having too many dogs in one apartment, I was very grateful for the hospitality that John and Peter offered Katie and me. In the dismal aftermath of 9/11, it was so comforting being together again.

We ate bagels and cereal in the morning as I talked to Ryan about his schoolwork. I strategized with John about my work and about functioning without my computer. And through it all, I gained enormous strength in their companionship, recapturing the closeness we'd always shared.

This was definitely not a time to be alone—and Granny was anything but happy marooned in New Jersey. She wasn't very close to her niece and nephew, Edith and Leonard, and felt somewhat uneasy in their home, as she later told me. But even if she had been comfortable, having been uprooted from her own apartment and traumatized by the physical rigors of 9/11, she was understandably depressed and anxious to be around her regular group.

"I miss the little child!" she told me yet again on the phone. "How's she doing?"

"Misbehaving, as usual," I laughed. "She's not very popular here with John's dogs—they hate her—and she's risking her life to steal their food."

"That's my girl!" laughed Pearl, who also missed her new friend, Lee, who had provided such kind and attentive care.

"Lee saved my life," Pearl told me gratefully, anxious to see her again.

Lee and I called Pearl every day, and, at first, she seemed okay. But she really wasn't. She seemed to resent the good intentions of her niece, mostly because she didn't want her independence taken away. So even though her niece got Pearl's hair and nails done, and bought her new clothes, which was certainly a kind thing to do, Pearl wanted none of it.

Pearl was becoming somewhat irrational and paranoid in her suburban surroundings. One day she called up telling me that she was locked up in the house, a "hostage," and couldn't get out, which was not the case. All this, I believed, was a function of being in shock—disoriented, crushingly lonely, and worried.

The solution was obvious: bring Pearl back to Manhattan, and fast. So John rented a car and, with Katie and Ryan in tow, off we went to Montclair to rescue her.

When we pulled into the driveway, Pearl rushed into our arms and gave us all a big hug, elated to be leaving for Manhattan. She looked good in a new shorter, curled hairdo and had obviously gotten excellent care. Katie was beside herself with excitement. She licked Granny's face and sat on her lap the entire way back into the city, a quick twelve-mile ride. She soon fell sound asleep in Pearl's arms, her paws hanging possessively over her wrists.

John and Peter didn't have room to host all of us, and I couldn't impose on them any longer than the two weeks I'd already stayed. Also, since Katie was so dissatisfied with being penned up all the time in the bathroom, it was definitely time for us to move out on our own.

Since FEMA was offering free hotel stays for all those displaced by 9/11, we searched for one that would take both people *and* dogs. The only dog-friendly hotel I could find was the Mayflower Hotel on Central Park West, right across from Central Park.

Unfortunately, they only had one room left, as the hotel was filled with many other displaced residents of Battery Park City. As much as I didn't want to be separated from Granny, I got her into the nearby Helmsley Hotel, around the corner from Carnegie Hall, just a few blocks from me and close to John and Ryan.

True, she was all alone in her room, but much happier.

"I'm free!" laughed Pearl, delighted to be back in walkable Manhattan, close to Katie and the gang. Most days, I picked her up for lunch and for dinner and we enjoyed long strolls in Central Park. Katie chased birds and squirrels as always and asserted herself, lunging at little dogs that irritated her.

Indoors, Katie reveled in her freedom and quickly made friends with the hotel maids. She followed them around, just as she had Ramon, hoping they might drop something to eat, which they never did. She marched through the lobby of the hotel and stopped to flirt with all the bellmen and anyone else willing to pet her. And even though she sometimes bumped into walls due to her cataracts, she was in good spirits, stimulated by the change of scenery while anchored to her "pack" of regulars—me, Pearl, John, and Ryan.

On October 7, we celebrated Pearl's eighty-ninth birthday at an Italian restaurant a few blocks from John's apartment. Rose was there along with Lee and other friends from Battery Park City, none of whom could yet return to our neighborhood, which remained off-limits and uninhabitable. Through the evening, Ryan snuggled close to Oldest, his head often touching hers as they posed happily for photos. Pearl looked radiant that night, smartly dressed in a black suit, a leopard-patterned blouse, and pearls. Ryan was so grown-up in a button-down blue dress shirt and khakis, his long bangs falling into his face.

We sang happy birthday off-key and had a chocolate fudge cake from the Cupcake Café, decorated with a wild garden of blue, red, and yellow sugar flowers. Granny took charge of cutting the slices, thinner than any of us would have liked. At the table, Ryan shoveled in cake as he showed Pearl his new Nintendo gadget.

As a birthday present, he gave Pearl a small plant for her

hotel room. "Thank you, sweetheart," she said, holding it as if it were made out of pure gold. "I love it."

That night as we headed back to our hotels, I realized something that I would never have fully understood had we not been displaced from our neighborhood: Home is not a place; it's the people placed in your heart.

So that night, even though Granny and I were still exiled from our homes, we were alive, and together again.

CHAPTER TWENTY

Ghost Town

I n late October, having been uprooted and living in hotels
since the terrorist attacks, Katie, Granny, and I finally
returned home, though our world, as we had known it, was
inexorably changed.

Although I, along with many other Battery Park City residents, had been briefly allowed into our building in late September to collect essentials (under National Guard escort), that
whirlwind visit had been a total blur.

We had been allotted exactly fifteen minutes to get in and
get out. "This is a crime scene," we were told, "and if you take
any photos, you'll be arrested."

I just rushed into my apartment and grabbed some clothes,
my checkbook, and files I needed for magazine stories, then
locked the door and got out, relieved to return to the hotel.

But before I left the neighborhood, I noticed two unmarked,
refrigerated trailers parked near our building. When I asked
one of the guardsmen about them, he told me that they held
human remains recovered at the disaster site.

And now, weeks later, on this crisp fall day, the trucks were still on site, morbid reminders that the cleanup was far from finished.

This was the day I actually *saw* the neighborhood again—and a sad sight it was.

It was hard to believe that just seven weeks earlier, the 110-story Twin Towers had been gleaming in the morning sunshine—hubs of commerce that dominated the landscape.

The skies were now vacant. What remained was a barren, flattened field filled with tons of twisted metal, powdery dust, armies of round-the-clock cleanup crews and, hidden from the eye, body parts still beneath the earth.

As we pulled up to our complex, Katie poked her nose out of the taxi window, curiously sniffing in the strange new smells. The streets were eerily empty. There was still a pungent smell of burning ash.

And as later reports revealed, even on the day of our arrival back home, the air was still toxic, polluted with asbestos and cement dust. By the furious swatting of her tail, however, Katie definitely knew she was home, though nothing was the same.

An aura of continuing shock and fear was palpable. Barricades blocked all nonessential traffic; trunks of cars were searched for bombs, while German shepherds sniffed every parcel and backpack. The community I'd known was like a war zone, and its residents, like war refugees, looked shell-shocked, with blank or dazed expressions, not a smile in sight.

As I looked beyond our circular driveway, mounted police navigated their horses around piles of debris, keeping a watchful eye on the temporary phone and electrical cables that were exposed aboveground. Portable toilets and hastily erected emergency telephone booths littered the once-manicured park adjacent to the Hudson River.

Most foreboding, police boats armed with machine guns patrolled the water, while Air Force helicopters hovered in the skies. Hearing the ominous sound of those helicopter blades, I wondered if we were returning home too soon—or if we should have returned at all.

On the way into our building, I stopped at our local drugstore to get a few supplies. Katie, as always, swiped a candy bar from the lower counter, which I plucked from her mouth, giving her my standard "no!" stare. Dejected, she slyly turned her head away from me, but stood ready, as always, to make another try.

As I walked back home on the near-empty streets, with no dogs or traffic, and almost nobody to keep us company, it struck me that our once-vibrant neighborhood—bustling with legions of babies, teenagers, young professionals, and seniors— was now a virtual ghost town.

Of the over 1,700 apartments in our complex, a whopping 70 percent of them were vacant. Many residents who had temporarily moved in with friends or family, or into hotels, were so shaken that they were never coming back. Some believed their children weren't safe, that with Wall Street so nearby, another attack was inevitable. Others suffered from posttraumatic stress and disappeared without even returning for their furniture.

But for Granny and me, Battery Park City was home, the place where our hearts would always be. And we would not be driven from it.

We had spent such happy days here together, outside in the park, walking with Katie along the water—surveying the sailboats, the marina, and sweeping views of the Hudson—eating ice cream on summer nights, enjoying outdoor concerts, and savoring the magnificent sight of the Statue of Liberty.

And inside our homes, we had baked cakes and cookies

together—eggs and sugar flying from one apartment to another. We had feasted on Granny's plum tarts and paprika chicken and breaded zucchini. We had shared holidays and Katie's annual birthday parties with her favorite carrot cake.

Through the rituals of celebration, we had established a true family unit that extended beyond just us to a wide network of our neighborhood friends—all of which made it impossible to even consider breaking it apart.

A friend living in another city asked why it had taken us so many weeks to get home. I explained that when one of the doomed planes flew into the Trade Center, one section of its wing had broken apart and been hurled, like a meteor, across the street, cutting a deep hole into the side of our thirty-five-story apartment tower, and shattering all the windows.

And so, on our first day back, as residents trickled back into the neighborhood, our homecoming was anything but happy. Yes, our homes were habitable, but everything was changed—and much was lost.

Tears flowed for all of us returning home that day, feeling, as we did, the ghostly presence of those now tragically gone.

❴⊐

As Katie and I entered the lobby of our building, I looked through the glass wall facing what had been a verdant backyard garden. It was now ripped up and brown. Seven weeks earlier, the grass had been covered with a blanket of singed papers hurled into midair during the implosion of the South Tower. The documents had been carried *across* the street from the burning towers, landing in our backyard. Also on the ground had been one stray shoe that had been blown from the foot of some poor soul. I had bent down to touch that shoe and had also found, nearby in the grass, a tube of lipstick and a banker's business card.

Although things had been cleaned up a little on that October day, our home, as we had known it, was definitely not the same. Our formerly pristine lobby, with its floor-to-ceiling mirrors, potted palms, polished steel columns, and Oriental carpets, was now dusty and disheveled, a shadow of its former self.

The sitting area was filled with the piles of luggage of returning residents. There were notices tacked to the walls about emergency services and apartment cleaning. Card tables set up in the area leading to the elevators were manned by FEMA workers and insurance representatives, who answered questions about resettlement efforts in Battery Park City.

Katie trotted over to one of the tables, spotted an open bag of Fritos lying under it, and efficiently swiped it, running to the elevator in an attempt to escape detection. She failed, as I grabbed it away and returned it.

A moment later, as Katie and I came off the elevator, she bounded happily down our long hallway, overjoyed to finally be back home in her territory.

"There's my girl!" Granny smiled with pleasure, as Katie ran into her arms, covering her face with kisses. "How's my little baby?!" she asked over and over again. Katie's tail told it all—just fine, happy to be reunited with Pearl.

∝∋

My feelings were somewhat ambivalent. Most of the apartments on our floor were deserted. The hallway was empty and dark, with only the dim emergency lights turned on.

Two weeks earlier, after the National Guard had loosened up its rules and allowed longer home visits, I had been able to return to my apartment to survey the damage. I was accompanied by my Travelers home insurance rep—a wonderfully warm woman named Jean Harper. An avid dog lover, Jean was seduced by Katie and was especially efficient in processing my claim.

"Wow, this really is depressing," I had told Jean as we

surveyed the mess inside. There had been considerable water and dust damage: The marble kitchen counter was cracked in two, the oak cabinets were warped, the light-beige marble floors had turned brown, the wallpaper was discolored, and the living room carpets permanently stained. Everything was soaked in an inch of yellowish water.

I was relieved to know that all of it would be repaired or replaced, though some things could never be. For example, my computer was a dusty wreck, destroyed by the refuse that had billowed inside on 9/11, blanketing everything with heavy black soot. Although I had backed up some of my files, much of what I had stored was permanently lost.

After that discouraging visit with Jean, I'd been consumed with having everything dried out and cleaned up before our arrival home. So a decontamination crew in spaceship-like uniforms had been brought in to scour every surface from floor to ceiling, removing the asbestos dust.

"This place really is a ghost town," whispered Pearl, startled by the shadowy hallway and the absence of her women friends, who were still scattered with friends and family.

As she was unpacking her things, she surveyed the thick dust covering every surface in her apartment, sad that most of her beloved plants were dead, except for one — the rhododendron given to her by Ryan.

She seemed overwhelmed by the cleanup task at hand, and I arranged for a cleaning company to decontaminate her apartment as well.

"I guess I'll go shopping for some food," she murmured that first day, setting off for the grocery store, walking down the stairs.

"Why don't you wait a minute — and I'll go down with you," I told her.

But independent as always, Pearl shook her head no, and walked right past me.

"I'm fine, don't worry."

But I was worried.

Oldest was definitely shaky (and who at her age wouldn't be?), off in her mood and energy, definitely not strong enough to resume her life as she had known it. But I gave her a lot of credit for trying.

Beyond the physical, I could see that the readjustment period was going to be difficult because she had recently grown reaccustomed to seeing Ryan and John nearly every day. But here she was downtown again, more alone than she wanted to be.

Meanwhile, Katie was oblivious to it all and trotted into my bedroom to find her favorite toy, the pink rubber mouse that squeaked when you squeezed it. She began shaking her head back and forth, tearing that thing apart with gusto. And then, as she always did, she picked up a sock and we played tug-of-war. Katie snarled enthusiastically as she attempted to rip it away from me.

Finally, she opened her mouth, her pink tongue hanging out, and gave me her version of a doggie smile, content, at last, to be home. I popped in a dog biscuit and she curled up on the couch and took a nap.

⟡

The next day, I called in Katie's beloved groomer, Betty, who had been cutting Katie's hair for thirteen years. Although De De's Dogarama had gone out of business a few years earlier, I was completely devoted to Betty, and she now made house calls.

"Hey girlfriend, I see you made it through 9/11, but your hair didn't!"

Katie ran into Betty's arms—enthralled to see her again. It

had been a long seven weeks in more ways than one, and anything we could do to reestablish a sense of normalcy was my goal.

Betty had always been such a down-to-earth gal and a true friend to Katie and to me. I relied on her for good advice about sundry things, whether it was discussing what "senior" dog food to purchase or the best cleanup sprays to counteract accidents.

I can still see Katie that day, patiently keeping her eyes shut tight as Betty briskly shampooed her dirty coat in the bathtub, the blackened water whirling down the drain. Then, Betty rinsed her with the hose attachment as Katie turned in circles, as if in a car wash, submitting to the pressure of the water. Later, during the haircutting phase of the operation, Katie, as always, had the good sense to hold up one paw at a time while Betty trimmed her nails and delicately cut the fur around her legs.

When Betty was finally done, there Katie stood, her old self once again—exquisitely clean, her blond hair so lustrous that it almost didn't look real. Betty swatted her on the butt, the sign that she was done, and Katie, relieved, scampered out of her reach into the kitchen for a reward.

CHAPTER TWENTY-ONE

Granny in the ER

We had much to be thankful for that Thanksgiving of 2001, finally safely home again. Pearl and I spent the holiday that year with Ryan and John, sharing a festive meal at the Marriott Hotel across the street from our complex ("all you can eat for $24.95, a great price," Pearl smiled, holding up the coupons for all to see).

That afternoon, Oldest, the matriarch of our little group, reminisced about the days her mother cooked Thanksgiving turkeys. Her secret for keeping the skin crispy was "dry brining the skin with salt!" she said.

She gave Peter her recipe for chestnut stuffing while Ryan polished off a meal big enough for two.

Life was slowly returning to normal as Pearl's cronies made their way back to the neighborhood. My across-the-hall neighbor, Freda, was back to formally greeting Katie, who carefully avoided her legs. Pearl's neighbor-to-neighbor girlfriends—Ruth, Bea, Sally, Sylvia, and Georgie—were back to sharing tea.

And not least important, Pearl's new friend Lee was kindly solicitous of her. She took her to the hairdresser, out to lunch, or for a walk, and checked in on her often as they reminisced about the unforgettable day they'd first met.

Even though Granny enjoyed it all (especially fussing over Ryan when she saw him and found out all about his school and new friends), her energy level was running low.

A week after the Thanksgiving dinner, Oldest had severe abdominal cramps and complained that she was "all blocked up," making a doctor's visit mandatory.

Although I wanted to accompany Pearl to the appointment, she refused. "I can do it. I'm fine," she again insisted. She trudged to the bus alone.

But two hours later, the doctor called, notifying me that Pearl had been hospitalized, taken directly from his office in an ambulance to Downtown Hospital, not far from Battery Park City. She was suffering from an intestinal blockage, the root cause being a severe case of diverticulitis. She needed immediate surgery.

"Oldest, Oldest Granny!" I exclaimed, holding her hand when I got into the ER, thinking back to the time when she had shown up for me after my bike accident. "What in the world are you doing in a place like this?"

"I'll do anything to take a nap."

"You look a lot better than I did when I was in the hospital."

"That's not saying much," she quipped, tart as always. "Now get me out of here."

"Not so fast, Grannsibel…here they come," I said, standing aside for the nurse who was about to prep Pearl for surgery.

A little while later, I followed Granny's gurney as she was rolled toward the operating room. "You'll be fine, Oldest," I said, holding her hand, "I'll be right here when you get out. And I'll bring Lee along."

"Do that," she said, squeezing my hand as they rolled her away.

But after the operation, Pearl was extremely weak and fighting a lung infection. Unable to breathe on her own, she was transferred into the Intensive Care Unit, put on a respirator, and kept sedated. Lee and I came by every day.

Honestly, it was heartrending to see Pearl in this condition, lying there helpless, pale, drained of strength, and in and out of consciousness for five days.

But when she was finally taken off the respirator, it didn't take long for her to perk up again. "Where's Lee?" she whispered, holding my hand when she first opened her eyes.

"She's right here," I said, ushering our cheerful friend into the room.

"Hi Pearlie Girlie," cooed Lee. A wonderful smile lit up her face as she took Granny's hand and bent down to give her a warm hug and kiss.

Pearl was thrilled. "How'd I get in this jam?" she cracked.

"We'll get you right out of it," Lee laughed, holding up a cup of water and putting the straw into Pearl's mouth for her to sip it.

I was encouraged by how quickly Pearl's inimitable humor resurfaced despite still being on painkillers. For example, there was a policeman stationed in the ICU, there to guard a prisoner in the cubicle next door. Pearl, who loved to flirt, kept glancing his way, batting her eyes and inviting him over to talk.

"Officer, I could use a little protection!" she giggled, discovering in conversation that he was of German ancestry. When he answered her with a few German words, Pearl responded to *him* in German—though she later claimed she never spoke it.

"Keep that gun handy," she whispered conspiratorially. "I don't trust anyone in this hospital."

Indeed, though she was often alert and in total command of

herself, at other times she was disoriented, sometimes even paranoid, a possible side effect from the anesthesia, we were told.

Once Pearl was released from the ICU and brought back up to a regular room, she was convinced, for example, that her roommate, an elderly Chinese woman, was trying to steal her money while she was sleeping.

"Granny," I told her. "She wouldn't do that. In fact, that woman can't even walk!"

"Well, I don't trust her," Pearl answered, handing me her wallet and instructing me to take it home with me.

Another time, she seemed to be hallucinating. "Where's Arthur?" she asked, grabbing my arm, certain he was still alive.

I believed that the quickest way to snap Pearl back to reality was to reunite her with you-know-who.

So I now did for Granny what she had once done for me—I snuck Katie into the hospital by camouflaging my dog, as always, in a big shopping bag, with a towel on top. Only her nose poked out from it.

"My girl is breaking the law!" Pearl laughed, elated to see Katie climbing out of the bag and onto her bed. Katie was all kisses and whimpered in joy before falling soundly asleep under the covers, hidden from the nurses. The two were blissfully content.

Granny spent another twelve days in the hospital. "She's doing very well," the doctor assured me, but I didn't agree. Yes, her infection was gone and the operation was declared a success, but Pearl wasn't the same as before she entered the hospital. Her speech was sometimes confused and she was extremely weak—certainly not the woman who, just a few years earlier, was walking briskly and doing all her own cleaning, shopping, and cooking.

It seemed to me that the events of 9/11 and the surgery that followed it had broken her.

It was finally time to leave the hospital—and we were all happy to be escaping it. In her undercover work as nurse's aide, Katie had done much to boost Pearl's spirits, snuggling in bed with her each day ("the best therapy," Pearl smiled). But it was obvious we couldn't take Granny home without first hiring an aide, as she could no longer care for herself.

She had once told me, "When I get to a certain age, *shoot me*." But we weren't going to do that, nor did we consider the idea of an assisted-living facility or a nursing home. Pearl was going *home*—though she was going to need lots of help.

Considering her independent spirit, the idea of depending on somebody else was going to be a major adjustment. As always, Pearl was stoic and made the best of things, but she didn't realize how drastically her life was going to change, literally overnight.

She now required help to do even the most basic things. She was unable to walk without assistance, and then only a few steps, so she was going to have to learn how to use a walker. Her hands shook so badly that she needed someone to cut up her food and feed it to her; and of course, she needed assistance in the bathroom too.

Katie seemed to sense Pearl's fragile condition. She gingerly licked her hand and lay against her in her hospital bed, though careful not to lie on top of her, as she had in the past.

I realized I couldn't function as Pearl's full-time aide, and it would have embarrassed us both for me to try. So the hospital's Social Services helped find a female aide to accompany us home to fill this function, at least temporarily.

Loretta was an experienced aide, a middle-aged woman who took her job seriously. On the day we left the hospital, she painstakingly helped Pearl get dressed and transferred her into the wheelchair, though Granny resisted her help from the minute she met her.

"Where'd you find this broad?" Granny whispered, a look of total disapproval on her face. "I don't care for her and neither will Katie."

Indeed, on the ride home, Pearl wouldn't even talk to Loretta, while Katie also ignored her. Over the next few days, Katie walked around Pearl's apartment with her tail down, unhappy with the intruder, while Pearl barricaded herself in her bedroom, never speaking to Loretta unless she absolutely had to.

"C'mon Granny, she's a nice woman and we need someone to help you," I told her.

"I'll send her down to your apartment and she can help *you!*"

One strike against Loretta was her bedside manner—way too bossy for Pearl, who was accustomed to being the boss herself. Understandably, Pearl hated being treated like a child and felt embarrassed to need help, especially in the bathroom.

Second, Loretta was no friend to Katie. She complained that my dog dripped water all over the floor and that having her around was "unsanitary."

"I won't clean up after her," she huffed. Nor would she feed Katie, a custom that my dog had long grown accustomed to.

Insensitive and rigid, Loretta failed to grasp the intense bond between Katie and Pearl, nor the therapeutic value of having Katie present.

Two weeks later, Loretta was gone.

Next was La-Teesha, a much younger woman who loved dogs and happily played with Katie (and overfed her) but spent most of her time on her cell phone, talking to her boyfriend. She wasn't very interested in Granny's care and treated her as a nuisance. We also found some of Granny's English Spode china in her tote bag. She lasted a week.

After these two mismatches, we finally hit gold with a woman from the Republic of Georgia, Naia, who had been a licensed physician in her native country and now worked as a nurse's aide in the United States. Georgia, I explained to Pearl, had been a Soviet Socialist Republic before the Soviet Union split apart.

"She a *Russian*?" asked Granny, suspicious of anyone I suggested after the last catastrophes. "A Communist?" she joked.

"Just meet her," I insisted, desperate to find someone right away. "We're very lucky to get her. She's actually a doctor."

"But does she like dogs?" Pearl asked. "I thought that first aide was going to cook Katie up into a stew for dinner."

"She loves dogs. Just meet her."

When I opened Pearl's front door the day of the interview, there was Naia, a beautiful young woman in her early thirties with long dark hair and magnificently arched eyebrows framing the most striking blue eyes I'd ever seen. As we talked, I was impressed by her seriousness and intelligence. And I was grateful to know that she could check Pearl's blood pressure and pulse, help her with physical rehab, monitor her medications, and easily get her in and out of the bed with no assistance. Not to mention the cooking and cleaning. She was a godsend.

Over the next few years, Naia would become a treasured member of our family—Katie's new keeper and the granddaughter that Granny never had.

But things were shaky at first. No surprise there. To put it politely, Pearl was aloof and not very receptive to Naia's help.

"But I tried not to take it personally," Naia later told me. "What I liked about Pearl was that she wasn't phony. What you saw was what you got."

I wasn't the easiest person to handle either, I admit. At first, I was overprotective and controlling, checking in too frequently to make sure that Pearl was being properly taken care of.

"Glenn was a bit bossy," Naia later told Lee. "But I admired his dedication. He used to come into the kitchen, open the refrigerator, and ask, 'Why isn't it full?' If I had one flavor of ice cream in the freezer, he wanted two. Everything was for Pearl. 'Take her to the movies, restaurant, hairdresser.' Glenn wanted everything perfect for her."

As the weeks rolled by, I was impressed by Naia, though Pearl still resisted her help and was predictably cold. Once she saw how capable she was in terms of medical care, however, she started complaining about her housekeeping and cooking.

"This place is a mess and she can't cook," huffed Oldest. "Did you *taste* that stew? They'd serve that in jail!"

I started laughing and couldn't stop.

A few nights later, after tasting the "foreign soup" that Naia had cooked up, Pearl was at it again. "This tastes weird," she scowled. "How about a matzo ball?" Naia soon caught on and made up lists of Pearl's favorite foods.

"I like chicken—nice and spicy," she ordered, but Naia refused, having been told by the doctor that Pearl could no longer eat spicy food.

"No Graaaaany," she told her, seamlessly adopting our pet name (and stretching it out just as we mispronounced it) for Pearl. "Not too much spice."

"Can you bake?" Granny asked.

"No, not really. But I'll buy you anything you want."

"Don't bother," she shrugged, "Glenn will do it," and off she went into the bedroom to watch TV, leaving Naia alone to ponder her difficult charge.

CHAPTER TWENTY-TWO

Georgia Peach

T hings were humming along perfectly.

Naia ran Pearl's household with great industry and was the most caring, meticulous aide anyone could ask for. I trusted her completely and was thankful for her attention to detail.

And it wasn't long before Oldest appreciated Naia too. Instead of merely tolerating her, Pearl began to genuinely like her—and they became friends. They took long walks on the Esplanade with Katie and spent hours in Pearl's bedroom— trying on clothes and jewelry, watching TV, talking about news and fashion, or paging through scrapbooks as Pearl reminisced about her early years with Arthur.

"After two or three months of working with her, it was fun," said Naia. "Pearl had a great sense of humor and was very sensitive to me. Some days when I was fighting with my boyfriend on the phone and was upset afterward, she always knew it (craftily eaves-dropping) and she'd try to cheer me up with little comments."

"Men are strange," Granny opined. "Don't get so upset about so little. If they're loyal and worth it, let them come back to you—like a dog; otherwise, let them off the leash!"

Then, without missing a beat, Pearl would pull out her ancient metal Land O'Lakes sweet cream butter box, where she kept her mother's prized recipes. "Let's try one," she'd say, and within minutes they were in the kitchen, baking a cake together as Katie sat on the floor, following their every move.

As their relationship developed, Naia did everything possible to improve Pearl's quality of life. Although Oldest had come back home from the hospital as an invalid, she regained her mobility thanks to Naia's encouragement and care. "Pearl could soon walk with no assistance, go to the bathroom, take a shower, and dress herself," said Naia. "I left the door open to her bedroom and kept an eye on her, but she was fine."

Having Naia on hand 24/7 allowed me to protect the essence of my relationship with Pearl as it had always been— conversational partners, confidantes, and neighborhood comrades-in-arms. All the other caretaking Naia did. Even though Pearl could no longer clean, shop for groceries, do the laundry, or go the doctor, bank, or dry cleaner alone, I think she secretly enjoyed the luxury of having someone do it all for her.

Part of Pearl's rehabilitation extended to updating her wardrobe and linens. "Granny is wearing old, ripped clothes," reported Naia. "Everything, including the towels, has holes in it." So I gave Naia a credit card and told her to start shopping, and off they went to Pearl's favorite store, Lochmann's—"great bargains!" Pearl enthused.

"One day, when we were at the store," Naia remembered, "I was looking at a wildly flowered blouse when Granny said, 'It's too busy.' I didn't understand what she meant. I didn't want to embarrass myself with my lack of English. And she kept repeating, 'It's very busy.' Finally, I asked, 'What *is* this busy?' She explained and we both laughed about it for days."

Girl talk now filled Pearl's apartment 24/7. One day, I

walked into Pearl's bedroom and saw that it had been turned into a salon. Pearl was on the bed, having her hair, nails, and makeup done by Naia, delighted with hot pink nail polish and the sensation of being primped and pampered. Katie sat on the bed alertly watching as Pearl had her hair set, curled, and blow-dried, something my dog was quite accustomed to.

"There's nobody like that girl!" Granny now bragged to all her older women friends, some of whom were jealous of Pearl's new "find."

And Pearl wasn't the only household member being seduced by Naia's charms. One night, just before bedtime, I let myself into Pearl's apartment to pick up Katie for the night. And there was my dog, sitting on Naia's lap, hypnotized as Naia sang a lilting lullaby to her—in Georgian! What a scene. Katie soon dropped her head on Naia's lap and fell asleep, Naia stroking her head like a baby.

Katie was entranced by Naia and followed her everywhere, as hopelessly in love with her as she was with Ramon.

And so, as if Pearl and I didn't lavish enough attention on Katie, Naia was now doing double duty, acting as Katie's aide as well—feeding her, cleaning out her water and food bowls, taking her on walks, brushing her ears, giving her vitamins and medicine, making special snacks for her, and kindly cleaning up after my fourteen-year-old when she had accidents.

"I love dogs, don't worry, it's nothing unmanageable," Naia assured me, fully aware of how therapeutic it was having Katie in Pearl's apartment. "Katie," she wisely surmised, "is Pearl's baby—but more like a queen."

After six months of intense involvement in our household, with all her industry, I could see that the stresses of the job—and homesickness—were getting to Naia. She sorely missed her family, all of them back in Georgia.

I worried about her, as did Granny. "That girl works too hard," Pearl told me. And I agreed, soon suggesting that she take weekends off. So we hired one of her Georgian friends as the weekend aide.

On Sunday nights when Naia returned, Katie practically leapt into her arms, racing around her in circles before trotting over to a living room cabinet and sitting still as a statue in front of it, staring at the Humpty Dumpty cookie jar where Naia kept her snacks.

Then, there we were, sitting around Pearl's table just like in the old days, though the players had changed. John and Ryan were gone, their chairs now filled by Naia and Lee—who visited almost every day.

Afterward, Katie scooted in Pearl's bed for an after-dinner snooze and a round of TV. I'd come by around 9:00 p.m. to gently lift her off the bed, say good night to Pearl and Naia, and then take Katie outside for her final walk.

At last, things were getting back to normal.

⌀

But by the summer of 2002, I was very worried about Katie. It seemed we were always going to the vet—she had an ear or urinary infection, an upset stomach, a sore hip, an infected paw, inflammation in her eyes, or she was listless with no appetite. You name it, she had it—and despite my furious attempts to keep her going, nothing was really working. It was wearing us both down.

Sometimes, though, Katie was almost like her old self again, bringing me toys and chasing squirrels outside; but more and more, she was out of gas and could hardly move, hiding in bed next to Granny and refusing to budge.

Now close to fifteen—which would be about eighty-three in human years—she relied mostly on smell and memory, and was nearly blind due to cataracts. Her vision was almost entirely blocked in her left eye, and only partially serviceable in her right.

"An operation is up to you," the ophthalmologist at the animal hospital had told me, "though at her age, you might just leave it alone."

It was really upsetting to see my incredibly intelligent dog disoriented and confused, her dignity bruised when she bumped into walls, producing a stunned look on her face.

"You're a good little girl, it's okay, now let's go this way," I said, guiding her toward the bedroom by keeping my hands on either side of her, then giving her a boost onto the bed, as she hobbled forward.

Katie was also going deaf, oblivious to her own name if you called it from behind, though she still willingly followed commands when she could hear them (most enjoyably, "over" for a belly rub). Like many canine seniors, she heard what she wanted to. When it came to a snack, of course, her ears pricked right up.

Most serious was Katie's arthritis, which made it painful, at times almost impossible, to walk. Some mornings, she would limp pitifully until she got warmed up and ready to move. More than once, she screeched out in pain when I tried to hitch up her leash and take her out for a walk, her legs collapsing under her. This was incredibly sad.

"My poor little girlie," whispered Pearl, looking distressed by all this as she sat nearby in her wheelchair. "We're both getting so old!"

On days Katie couldn't walk at all, I'd carry her to the street as I did when she was a baby, gently setting her down on the pavement, waiting for her to go. More and more, she couldn't even squat because her legs were too weak to hold her weight.

Inside the house, she'd stumble on the way to her food dish, though anxious to get there. And even when I picked her up to take her back into bed, she was so fragile that she would wince at my touch.

In short, seeing Katie so frail, and witnessing her steady deterioration, was devastating. It broke my heart to see a dog who had once raced through the park and leapt on and off the bed like a gymnast now reduced to limping her way to the door, her wobbly legs barely able to support her.

Even worse, Katie, who had always been perfectly house-broken, was now often incontinent, wandering into the living room at night to relieve herself. Sometimes, at 3:00 a.m. I'd find her in the midst of it all—and to my regret, I sometimes lost patience with her. I can still see her desperately remorseful expression. "*I'm sorry. I didn't mean to do it, Dad. Please forgive me.*"

And with her tail down, she would slink off to the marble floor of the bathroom, knowing that she should stay away from the carpet. I'd find her curled up on the cold tile, shivering, her head tucked into her front paws.

When I walked in to take her back into the bedroom, she looked up at me so astutely, her eyes expressing the sadness we both felt.

Yet, during that summer, even though Katie was ailing, she still liked going outside at sunset to relax by the water. Most nights, I'd choose a bench just a few feet from the river's edge opposite the Statue of Liberty, and she'd contentedly sit on my lap, snuggling in against me.

With the wind blowing her ears, Katie would extend her head toward the water and sniff away, curious as ever. And as sailboats caught the wind and glided by, Katie enjoyed the breezes, her tail wagging as she accepted pats on the head from her friends passing us.

Then, with the sun sliding down the sky and the temperature dropping, she'd shiver and bury her head in my arm, or take cover under my jacket, with just her head poking out of it.

I'd often talk into her ear, telling her what a good girl she was, using some of her favorite words. Sometimes, when I was in the middle of a sentence, she'd turn her head and quickly lick my face, up and down, as if to say, "*Dad, I love you.*" This was the greatest sensation—better than the view.

Sharing that bench together at sunset, feeling her weight against me, was peaceful and meditative, the best part of the day. I loved my dog so much and felt as protective of her as if she'd been a baby, especially now, when she was so fragile and in pain.

After nearly fifteen years together, the bond between us was something beyond words. So on those magical nights at sunset, I savored our moments together under the linden trees and wished they could last forever.

During that summer of 2002, Oldest, whose health had been stable, was suddenly acting strangely—disoriented and increasingly confused.

Some days, alone in her bedroom, she would talk to an ancient hand-painted porcelain doll (one leg broken) that she had treasured as a little girl. On and on, she would tell the doll her sweet secrets, sharing her fears of the dark and her thoughts about everything from the weather to the stock market.

On other days, she'd be having conversations with her deceased mother or Arthur, pointing toward her bedroom closet, telling me that they were hiding in there.

Sometimes, thankfully, she was completely lucid. You just never knew. Was this senile dementia or something more?

It turned out to be both. We learned that summer that Pearl had a benign, slow-growing brain tumor. Although it wasn't necessary to remove the growth, I was told that it would very gradually make her overall mental functioning worsen. "God," sighed Lee, "as if that poor woman hasn't gone through enough."

We didn't tell Pearl about the tumor, figuring it would serve no purpose. She was finding it difficult enough just to function day-to-day. I did, of course, discuss Pearl's medical condition with her family. Although Pearl wasn't particularly close to Edith, the niece she'd stayed with after 9/11, she did periodically keep in touch with her and appreciated what she had done for her during those difficult days.

I was glad to see that Pearl's grand-niece, Susan, and grand-nephew, James, continued to be a source of joy for Pearl. Although they were not close by, with Susan in London and James in Boston, Pearl delighted in their phone calls, notes, and visits. We were always hearing stories of how sweet they were and about their accomplishments. James and his mother, Edith, had attended Pearl's eighty-fifth birthday party at my apartment, and I periodically kept them updated on Pearl's health as they were quite concerned about it.

And as Pearl became progressively worse, I'd often reach out, especially to James, to brief him about her treatment. In the end, though, being unavailable to provide hands-on care, Pearl's relatives came to largely depend on me—together with Naia—as Pearl's primary support system, figuring that all was basically well while we were around. Clearly, keeping Pearl at home in Battery Park City was far preferable to putting her in an assisted-living facility or in a nursing home.

Her moods, however, were now volatile and unpredictable. After a psychiatric consultation, Pearl was given prescriptions for a tranquilizer, an antidepressant, and antianxiety medication. True, she was no longer as nervous or panicky, but now she was so doped up with the pills that she spent most of her time in bed, sound asleep or dozing.

Naia was more actively involved in nursing Pearl than ever, expertly juggling the array of prescribed pills. She often ground them up and put them into her food, as Pearl found it difficult to swallow them.

"She was better physically than mentally," Naia observed. "She still had great posture, and wonderful manners—and I envied her strength."

To Katie, of course, Granny's state of mind made absolutely no difference. She burrowed in right next to her, keeping her warm and snuggling mornings and nights, happy to be close.

As the months passed, Granny and Katie spent more and more time in bed sleeping the day away, their long afternoon naps extending late into the day. It was so poignant seeing them together, both aging and ailing, but still bonded for life.

Katie may have lost her vision, her hearing, and her energy for going outside, but she never lost her love for Granny— or me.

That fall, thanks to the medication, Granny's mood suddenly stabilized and her spirits slowly revived. We all started laughing again. As always, Lee came by every single day—and Pearl loved it. They talked for hours at a time, either in her bedroom or at our local coffee shop just a block away.

Even though Pearl was old enough to be Lee's mother, they related as if they were complete contemporaries. Although Pearl was sometimes confused, she was no less opinionated than before and offered her views about everything.

"Why do all these girls walk around naked in the middle of the fall?" was one of Pearl's frequent questions, referring to the army of joggers on the Esplanade. "In my day, even hookers had more clothes on. What happened to good manners?"

"Beats me," laughed Lee.

"George Bush," she observed one day, "is suddenly a *hero* [thanks to 9/11], but I still think he's a *zero*"—her astute assessment of him borne out by many political pundits.

One night in early fall, I pulled out a Donald Duck hat I'd purchased for Pearl at Disney World twelve years earlier.

"Remember this, Oldest?" I asked Granny, handing it to her.

She happily put on the hat, looking absolutely ridiculous in it as she nonchalantly chatted away with Lee before breaking into giggles. Katie looked up quizzically, wondering about that odd thing on Granny's head.

"I've seen worse hats, though I've looked better in them," Pearl said, mugging for the camera as I snapped away. Later on, the photos reminded me that, even in her weakened state, Granny never lost her game spirit or her wit. On her worst day she was more fun than many people were on their best.

One evening, she was visiting with a friend of mine who had a constant battle with the bulge. "You look thinner," she told him.

When I came into the room, he joyfully turned to me, and said, "Granny says I look thin."

Pearl shot him a look, and retorted, "I didn't say that. I said you look *thinner*."

That was our Granny!

CHAPTER TWENTY-THREE

Nocturne

In late 2002, as Indian summer turned to fall in Battery Park City, Katie was really struggling. Ever since 9/11, she had become increasingly frail and the old mischief and bounce were unmistakably fading away. On our walks outside along the marina, even when it wasn't cold, she often shivered and was out of breath, no longer very interested in the birds or squirrels.

I felt terrible as she just limped along, trying her best to walk despite the pain in her legs and inability to see or hear. We were both battling against the inevitable.

For months, I'd been trying to patch together another good day for her, but it wasn't working. Her moments of tail-wagging, snatching up her toys, playing tug-of-war, or smiling up at me with her tongue hanging out were over. Some days she wouldn't even go near her food bowl.

As a senior citizen of the dog world, Katie's sadness had only increased with her physical infirmities. Her beautiful brown eyes were swollen and bulging due to fluid buildup. Only able to see blurs and shadows, she was bumping into walls more and more. It was pitiful. And her failing hearing only exacerbated the problem.

Most of the time, her inability to hear me except when I was right in front of her face seemed to put her in a fog. She wandered aimlessly around the apartment, often in circles.

Of course, her nose and memory never failed and she always knew when Naia was frosting a cake, lying patiently on the kitchen floor waiting for a lick of the spoon. This was a pleasure she could still enjoy.

But making matters worse, she was now almost entirely incontinent, an indignity that I know she hated. She'd always been in control of herself and extremely clean. But now, after every accident, her tail went straight down, her head hanging low to the ground in defeat. The lethargy of her demeanor spoke volumes, her depression evident in the droop of her head.

In short, without her vision or hearing, and barely able to walk, she had lost interest in life, content to sleep the days away. I knew what was coming, though I didn't want to contemplate it.

Euthanasia was a prospect that the vet had suggested more than once over the last few months, but I was fighting it. I would have preferred waiting until Katie had a natural passing, all on her own. But I was told that that was not the humane thing to do when a dog is in constant pain and in failing health. One part of me saw the wisdom in ending my dog's misery, while the other thought I should wait and let nature take its course. After all, Katie didn't have a terminal illness or cancer, though she was often in severe pain due to the arthritis.

Naturally, I had talked with Pearl about it as much as I could—but she was firmly opposed to having Katie put to sleep. "She's not ready yet," Granny said stubbornly, her expression filled with fear and a sense of profound sadness. I sometimes wondered if she was talking about Katie or herself. I think she understood that Katie was ready to go, but, even so, it was impossible to say good-bye.

But by November of that year, I could no longer avoid the decision about euthanasia, as Katie was barely able to move at all, her interest in life seemingly gone. And so, with dread, I had finally made up my mind.

The morning of November 19 was cold and blustery. Granny had had a restless night and had taken a sleeping pill, which finally knocked her out. "She can't get up," Naia told me. And I was relieved, as I desperately wanted to avoid this farewell.

The night before, Katie had had a good time with Pearl, eating from her plate and licking her face over and over again. I thought maybe it was best to leave it this way and gently break the news later, sparing Granny the pain of a final good-bye.

So early that morning, I asked Lee to accompany me to the vet's office, intending to put Katie to sleep. I couldn't quite believe I was going to do it—but knew I couldn't face it alone.

Lee was pale as we got into a taxi, tears filling her eyes. She was opposed to my decision, though she respected it. As she later told me, "On the way up to the doctor's office, you had Katie on your lap and you were crying too. I wasn't sure what you were going to do." Truthfully, neither was I.

In the taxi, Katie slept in my arms, her head falling over my wrist. She was oblivious to her surroundings.

"She's very thin," the vet told me, "twenty-one pounds, down from twenty-eight. That's a lot." She was so weak she couldn't stand on the exam table, and the vet gently held her as he listened to her heart. He then calmly explained the procedure for euthanizing a dog. I hated hearing it and felt panicked.

After listening to all of it, I said, "No, I can't do it." And I'll never forget his answer, "I think she's ready, but you're not."

And it was true. I just couldn't do it.

On the way out of the vet's office, I optimistically bought a twenty-pound bag of Katie's favorite dog food—Prescription Diet.

When we got home from the vet, I carried a very drowsy Katie into the elevator and up to the third floor. Once we got in the hallway, though, she perked up and squirmed out of my arms, pressing onward toward Granny's half-open door. Whereas she used to easily push it open with both paws, she now scratched against it weakly, her breath heavy.

A few days earlier, desperately needing someone to talk to about the prospect of putting Katie to sleep, I had turned to my lifelong friend, Paul, whom I'd first met in college at a conservatory of music where we'd both been aspiring concert pianists. He had stuck with it; I didn't and became a writer.

Paul was a very calm, steady force in my life, a philosopher at heart who was a great support during this time. He offered to come down from Boston for a few days to help out.

Granny adored the handsome Paul (an amateur bodybuilder) and flirted shamelessly with him. During his summer visits, they would talk for hours and often went on long walks along the Hudson River holding hands. Katie also loved Paul and would nap for hours with her head on his foot or stomach, and she typically refused to sleep with me on nights he was visiting.

Paul was also a devoted dog owner who had euthanized his beloved Cleo, a Lab-Doberman mix, two years earlier, so he understood the agonizing conflict about putting a dog to sleep, a subject we had talked about frequently by phone.

"Howdy," whispered Paul, who arrived at my door later that very day with just his backpack and a small box of dog biscuits for Katie. It was fantastic seeing him again, looking robust and energetic as always. Katie was resting under the coffee table in the living room and opened just one eye as Paul walked into the room. Her tail started wagging as her nose identified him.

"Hello, girl," said Paul, bending down to play with her. She was lethargic, sleepy, and mostly unresponsive, though she gave him one long lick on his cheek.

"Wow," exclaimed Paul, struck by the drastic deterioration in Katie since the time he'd seen her eighteen months earlier. "She's a tired little soldier."

She fell back asleep on his lap.

"You know," Paul told me as he gently stroked her head, "having worked at a nursing home, Katie's demeanor reminds me of some very elderly people I knew. As people get near the end, there's a kind of gauzy veil that comes down between them and everyday reality. Their reactions are slow and not quite appropriate—almost as if they already have one foot on the other side.

"Based on my perception of Katie," Paul continued, "she is ready to go. I probably would have done it a little sooner."

I told Paul about what had happened at the vet earlier that day. He understood why I had changed my mind about euthanasia, though our conversation about it made me believe that I had made the wrong decision.

"You know what? Tomorrow morning, if you'll go with me, I'm going to try again. I do think you're right. It's time."

"Whatever you decide," Paul said, his arm around my shoulder, "I'm there."

That night, Katie seemed revived, much more energetic, which only made me doubt my decision once again. A group of us all had dinner at Granny's apartment—Paul, Naia, Lee, and I. It was a lively happy evening, just like the old days. I balanced Katie on my lap at the table as Granny fed her bits of chicken, some rice, toast, and a little pound cake. Although Katie couldn't see, she ruled that dining table with the same authority as always and had a great appetite, licking frosting off Granny's hand.

The next morning began deliciously, with Katie burrowed under the heavy down comforter, snoring away softly as she leaned into my chest, warm as a little oven.

An expert snuggler, Katie had her wet black nose pressed up against me, and those comically long spaniel ears draped across one of my arms. I never tired of having her next to me. Waking up next to Katie, even after all these years, was incredibly comforting. Her mere presence—the powdery smell of her warm little belly—could wipe away a bad dream or any lingering worry.

But on this day, I was feeling anything but good, dreading the day and what it would bring. Katie's familiar presence was bittersweet and haunting—and I hated the idea of taking her back to the vet. Even though I had vowed that today would be the day, I still wasn't 100 percent sure. A stab of panic went through me as I tried to wrap my mind around the idea that this was the last morning of Katie's life, the last time we'd ever wake up together again.

On many mornings, especially when she was in the midst of a happy dog dream, Katie would often wake *me* up with the swat of her tail against my stomach, her eyes—framed by those long blond lashes—blissfully sealed shut.

But now, with her joints so stiff, she understandably was immobilized under the sheets.

"Come on, Katie," I whispered, nudging her gently. "Ready to go?"

In healthier days, she'd play a game: just one eyelid would open, slyly, then quickly close again, her decision firm.

It was her way of saying, "*No way, Dad, I need my rest!*" She'd then playfully slide farther down the bed, head pointed down toward my feet.

But now, she wasn't moving at all, though she was breathing peacefully.

Katie had always been a regal dog, headstrong and imperious, and seeing her weak and vulnerable was heartbreaking. Yet I knew she had to go outside to relieve herself. Although I intended on carrying her, I first had to get her in a coat so she wouldn't freeze on the cold November day. Again, I tried to get her to sit up in the bed by raising the pitch of my voice into a seduction that had always worked in the past.

"Come oooooon, doggie. You can do it!"

She briefly opened her eyes, but slid further away. "*No!*"

It would have taken an entire cake rather than just a cookie to rouse her, for sleep was her great pleasure.

Eventually, she surfaced from beneath the sheet, only her nose above it, stretched up a bit, and licked my nose as she yawned lazily in my face. Her mouth was wide open, as if to say, "*Dad! I'm too tired to move. I can't.*"

But always such a good girl, she finally sat up on the bed and waited for me to get her ready. She held up her paws, one at a time, compliantly slipping them into the "arm" holes of her pink wool coat, resigned to the inevitable trip outside, this time with Paul keeping us company.

I scooped Katie up, took her downstairs in my arms, and we went out into that gray, chilly day. I gently set her down on the pavement. But she simply froze. She couldn't move at all. She just stood there, still as a statue, shivering and staring into space, making no attempt to relieve herself. Her dazed, disoriented expression said it all, "*I can't go. I just can't.*"

Although I obviously knew she was in very bad shape, this

was the first time this had ever happened. I leaned down to her, stroking her head, "Katie, come on, you can do it. *Go ahead.*"

Over the years, the phrase *go ahead* had become a mantra that I had repeated hundreds of times. This was her cue to get down to business and she always complied—but not now.

She just looked up at me hesitantly, her eyes glazed over, so vulnerable—and trusting. "*Please take me home.*"

So I gently picked her up.

I knew I'd made the right decision after my talk with Paul yesterday.

This was the end.

⋙

Before Paul and I went off, I carried Katie into Granny's apartment for the last time. I rethought my desire to avoid this farewell, horrible as it would be. No toast was waiting for Katie at the corner of the dining table, as it usually was. Naia was out at the grocery store. And Pearl was in bed under the tan-and-orange afghan that her mother had knitted for her decades earlier. It was time to say good-bye.

I lifted Katie up and placed her right on top of Granny. "How's my sweet baby girl?" Pearl asked, cooing with pleasure, though weak due to continued difficulties with her stomach.

"Not too good, Oldest," I answered. "Katie is really weak today. She can't walk. She can't 'go.' She just can't do anything…" My voice trailed off. And hoping she wouldn't hear me, I said, "I think it's time…"

Pearl was such a sturdy, practical woman, even at age ninety, and I had never seen her cry, except at Arthur's funeral eight years earlier. But now, tears were streaming down her face as she stroked Katie's head and held her close.

"Oh, no…you can't…not my girl…" she whispered. I turned away, about to lose it completely. Seeing the two of them together in these final moments was worse than I thought it would be. They were soulmates who'd been together for nearly fifteen years.

Katie snuggled close to Granny, her eyes shut, happy to be close.

I didn't know how I was going to get Katie off Pearl. I couldn't wrest them apart.

Granny didn't say another word. We just sat there silently, crying, both holding the dog that had drawn us together and kept us together for so many years.

Then I lifted Katie up and took her down the hall for the last time. "Wait!" Pearl ordered. "Let me kiss her." And as we bent back down, Katie licked Granny a final time.

Paul was waiting for us and I handed Katie to him. As he cradled her in his arms, I took a final photo of the child. She looked so sweet and vulnerable. Her face was thin, almost shrunken, but her beauty remained intact. Even in her pain, her spirit reached out to me, offering the kind of wisdom and comfort that only dogs can give. It was as if she was saying, *"Dad, don't worry. You've taken real good care of me—and now I'm ready."*

A few minutes later, we again set off in a taxi to the vet's office, Katie sleeping peacefully in my arms.

The vet, sensitively, had made sure that he had a large block of time so that he wouldn't be rushed by other appointments. He carefully explained that he was first going to give Katie a painless injection under her skin, a sedative that would make her relaxed and calm, sending her into a twilight sleep.

Katie was shivering, looking up at me plaintively.

"Dad, what's going on?"

I whispered in her ear something I'd been repeating for years, "You're a good girl...such a good, good girl. You're going to be fine." And I kissed her on her nose and hugged her close.

After the first injection, sure enough, within just a few minutes, Katie was sleeping soundly in my arms, just as she'd been earlier that day. I leaned down and savored the familiar sweet smell of her. My baby was at peace.

Then I carried her into the room where she had always had her checkups. And there, in the center of it, was that steel examining table that, to me, was like an executioner's booth. I remember thinking that there should be a soft towel or cushion on top of it, that its surface was too hard and cold.

As I laid Katie down on the table, the vet promised me that the euthanasia solution into her vein would be painless, and that within six to twelve seconds, it would take effect.

Just before he gave the shot, I put my left hand under Katie's warm stomach and the right one against her heart. I bent over and leaned in close as the needle went in. "Good girl..."

Katie took a deep breath. I could feel her heart beating, but within just a few seconds, it stopped. She was gone, her chest silent.

I had listened to her breathing for so many years, but now there was nothing. Katie's once-animated face—which had remained so beautiful—was now strangely sunken in...and still.

"I'll leave you alone for a few minutes," the vet whispered, and he closed the door.

I couldn't wait for him to leave. My entire body was vibrating. I bent over and gave Katie such a snug hug with my face and chest, stroking her back, telling her what a good girl she'd always been, and how much I loved her.

I couldn't stop crying. My little dog's body was still warm...

but she was gone. I kissed her nose and, for a final time, stroked her beautiful head, which was now resting on her paws.

I didn't want to leave Katie behind on that horrible table. After fifteen years, this was it. I'd never see Katie again. I felt like I was abandoning her.

I stayed a few minutes longer, with my hand gently stroking her back, and then forced myself to turn away. And as I left the room, I wondered if I'd made a mistake, if I should have waited longer for this day. This thought would haunt me for years.

I can tell you that if I could turn back the clock and have Katie home again for a week, a day, or for even an hour—I would give anything to do it. *Anything*.

After I left Katie and walked back into the reception area, the casual conversation of the secretaries and the ringing of phones startled me back into a different dimension.

How strange. I just left my dog and here I am handing over my American Express card to pay a fee for having her put to sleep. It was surreal.

I asked the vet and his assistant if they would be very gentle with Katie's body, and that they not take her away until I had left the building. I didn't want to think about what they were going to do with her.

I had chosen cremation and had declined receiving the ashes, feeling that having them would provide little comfort. After all, an urn of ashes was not the same as Katie. Yet, a few years later, I admit I would have liked to have had them. Instead, though, I have dozens of scrapbooks and hundreds of photos that bring her back to life, reminding me of her sweet spirit.

Afterward, the taxi ride home with Paul was desolate. I sat there holding Katie's red collar, leash, and gold-engraved ID tag.

"As painful as it is to lose Katie, or any dog," Paul told me,

"I always remind myself that our dogs want us to be happy. They live for it. Knowing this, more than anything, I think, is the secret to accepting the loss."

Paul was right, and his words would come back to me for months to come, helping me recover.

When I got back and went into Pearl's bedroom to share with her what had happened, she just closed her eyes, murmured a sigh of regret under her breath, and then rolled over toward the window so she wouldn't have to deal with it.

Yet that night, her spirits revived a bit when she heard that John and Ryan were coming over for dinner, bringing a rotisserie chicken, one of her favorites. It's funny how, even at the saddest times of our lives, we still get hungry. We all sat together that night, recounting the things we loved most about Katie. I can never forget Ryan placing his hand so sweetly on top of mine to console me, then coming over and putting his cheek against mine for a big hug.

"That's my boy!" exclaimed Granny with pride.

A few feet away, sadly, were Katie's water and food bowls, set out, as always, on her plastic Walt Disney placemat. We just left them there.

Later that night, Paul and I hatched what we thought was a great idea. To celebrate Katie, why not give a special memorial concert? We would *both* play the piano, and I knew that jumping into something like this would be good therapy.

So over the next few days, I sent e-mail invitations, made phone calls, called a caterer and a bakery, and enlisted the always helpful Lee to coordinate it.

Meanwhile, I practiced the piano furiously, willing my stiff, out-of-shape fingers to get back into condition and reviving those muscle reflexes needed for a Chopin nocturne and two movements of Chopin's Funeral March Sonata. Paul, always ready to perform, would play some Mozart, Debussy, and Chopin.

Katie had so many friends—a colorful cast of people she'd known over the years—that we wound up having two evenings of music, thirty people at each, with neighbors, friends, and family sitting on every available chair, cushion, and window ledge.

One of our neighbors on our floor, Geraldine, charmingly Irish and warm-hearted, practically emptied her living room of chairs to help out. There was candlelight in the room. Decorating the piano was my favorite framed picture of Katie in her sequined dress and a birthday hat on her head.

One of Katie's greatest fans was our longtime doorman Teddy, who moonlighted as a pastor at his local Baptist church. Teddy set such a moving tone for the evening, tenderly beginning with a prayer of thanks about how blessed we had been to have Katie and how much we all loved her.

"Katie's tender spirit will always be with us—as a comfort to us," Teddy said. "And we will never forget the way she brought us all together—how much love she gave even when she herself was in pain. She wasn't just a dog—she was a member of our family." With a grin, he added, "And she'd hate to be missing all this delicious food!"

There, in the front row, was Granny, proudly sitting with all her favorite friends (most of them in their late eighties and early nineties)—Sylvia, Georgie, Ruth, Bea, Freda, and Gloria. Equally touching was a contingent of *dogs*—all of them stretched out on the carpet. In addition to Jake, the German shepherd, there was Freemont, a Wheaten terrier; Clayton, a Labrador retriever; and Fred, a bichon frisé. Alas, there was no room for Katie's friend, Walter, the horse!

Amazingly, Katie's canine friends were completely attentive, hardly moving as the little recital unfolded. In the "funeral march" of Chopin's B-flat Minor Sonata, there's a lyrically pastoral section in the middle, my favorite. And as I played the melody—with the lucid tone of that Steinway piano filling the room—I glanced up at that picture of Katie in her birthday hat—and the tears came.

I just kept going, thinking to myself that my dog was now in heaven—and that we were all giving her a great, musical, farewell. As I was playing, I realized that I could express my feelings for her better through my fingers than with words. And as the music filled the room, there was an amazing sense of camaraderie that made this a happy night, rather than a sad one.

And so it was that Katie had the most fantastic send-off—an overflow crowd, her favorite friends and family together, John and Ryan and her beloved Granny—all remembering one little remarkable dog and the magnificent spirit that she had left behind.

That night, as I got into bed, I was exhausted yet oddly exhilarated—deeply satisfied at the memory of what had been.

At one point during the night, I heard the table skirt rustle next to me—just as it had with Katie playing under it—and only half awake, I believed she had come back.

Turning the light on, I found a gift from Paul on the night table, a wonderful little book written by Eugene O'Neill, titled: *The Last Will and Testament of an Extremely Distinguished Dog.* * The narrative is written in the voice of a departed dog who offers his grief-stricken owner words of comfort, reminding humans to be happy.

I ask my Master and Mistress to remember me always, but not to grieve for me too long. In my life I have tried to

---

* Henry Holt & Company, 1999.

be a comfort to them in time of sorrow, and a reason for added joy in their happiness. It is painful for me to think that even in death I should cause them pain.

Toward the end of the book, the dog writes that his memory should bring nothing but joy, that when we visit the grave, we should remember that the love that ties us together has no end:

No matter how deep my sleep I shall hear you, and not all the power of death can keep my spirit from wagging a grateful tail.

CHAPTER TWENTY-FOUR

"Have a Great Time"

"And Call Me!"

The morning after Katie's second memorial concert, Pearl was up and around having toast with Paul and me at her dining table, chatting quietly about the evening as she passed around lox and cream cheese, her favorites.

"Last night was *wonderful*," she said proudly, putting her hand on Paul's shoulder. She complimented him on his piano playing while urging him to take another piece of fish.

"But what," she asked plaintively, "am I going to do without my girl?"

That was the question.

"Well," Paul reflected, munching slowly, as he always did, savoring his food as he carefully chose his words, "at the time my dog, Cleo, died, I was reading a great book titled *A Hole in the World*—and I remember feeling that emptiness inside me. The bottom just fell out of my world."

Granny looked up and concentrated on Paul, as she took what he had to say seriously.

"It hit me harder than the death of any person I'd known," he admitted. "That's how important Cleo was to me. I cried a lot, for a long time, and rode the wave and let time take the edge off the pain, rather than resisting it.

"And," Paul added, "dogs who are devoted to their owners have been known to go to heroic lengths to hide their own pain and to protect them from distress.

"So the sadness we feel," he finished, "is a price worth paying for the joy that our dogs give us while they're living. I always try to remember how lucky I was having her with me as long as I did."

"You're right, you are," agreed Pearl, her voice trailing off. Paul was logical and comforting, but from the sad expression on Pearl's face, I could see that nothing was going to make much of a difference right now.

But one thing he had just said stung me, ringing painfully true. Toward the end of her life, Katie would often hide in the bathroom and lie on the cold floor, her head turned sideways; she was so miserable but was determined to keep me away from her pain. Finding her this way broke my heart every time. I'd gently pick her up, whispering into her ear what a good girl she was as I put her back into my bed against the down pillows.

During this visit, Naia came over to the table and stroked Pearl's hand, as she often did now.

"Something weird happened last night," I told Granny. "At one point during the night, I heard the table skirt rustling next to the bed—just as it did when Katie was playing under it—and I swear, I thought it *was* Katie—until I woke up."

"Your girl loved hiding under that table—and ruined the skirt! Remember?"

I sure did. And it was worth every trip to the dry cleaner.

Breakfast was over and Oldest got up and returned to bed, although it was early in the morning.

A few hours later, Paul was about to say his good-byes, ready for the return trip to Boston. Just before he left, the anticipation of being alone again left me with a homesick, sinking feeling. I wasn't ready to see him go. My friend of thirty-two years had been with me for this last chapter of Katie's life—and with me at the piano too.

He wrapped me in a fierce hug. "You're going to be fine, you are, just fine, even without Katie." I wasn't so sure.

I went back into Granny's apartment, but she was still hibernating under the covers, sound asleep. She'd stay that way most of the day. Sleep was her great escape, and I envied it.

"Katie was her baby," said Naia, sipping a steaming cup of herbal tea as we sat together at the table. "She gave her a reason to live." Just as Ryan had, I thought to myself.

Although I didn't know it at the time, Pearl was pouring her heart out to her dear friend Rose more and more, though she kept her emotions in check around me, "Pearl was sick when you put Katie to sleep," Rose later told me.

That wasn't exactly what I needed to hear. I knew Pearl was opposed to my decision for euthanasia and I felt horribly guilty about it—continually second-guessing myself about it. Had I done the right thing at the right time?

"Of course you did," Rose assured me, knowing full well how Katie had been suffering.

But without her now, a great vacuum was left behind. Everything I looked at in Pearl's apartment reminded me of "the child." There was the dining chair that she sat on as she mischievously stole food off Granny's plate, efficiently eating row after row of corn on the cob; strewn on the floor were her leftover toys, including her favorite squeaky mouse; sitting on the cabinet was that Humpty Dumpty cookie jar, still filled with Milk-Bones; etched on the door were all the happy scratch marks from her paws; and sitting deserted on the floor were her Disney-character water and food bowls, her Minnie Mouse rubber placemat under them. I quietly picked them up and started back home.

To say our hallway was quiet was an understatement. As I walked slowly down the corridor, my mind was flooded with a kaleidoscope of images, spread out over nearly fifteen years.

I could see Katie merrily skipping behind me, eagerly jumping up on my legs as we made our way to Pearl's. There she was, retrieving the blue rubber ball thrown by Arthur or cheating Ryan at the starting line by jumping the gun. I saw her running wildly to the elevator to greet Ramon, throwing herself on her back for a belly rub, legs straight in the air. There she was, strutting between apartments in her party dress, her wagging tail sticking out from the ruffles of black satin.

When I opened my apartment door, all the emotions I'd been feeling in the last few days caught me in the throat. I'd held back most of them, occupied with the vet, Pearl, Paul, and the memorial—existing on adrenaline and chocolate, with little sleep.

But now, alone, I let go. Once I started crying, I couldn't stop. I made it to the living room and when I saw Katie's favorite green chair with one of her toy rabbits left on its cushion, the pain of her loss sliced through me. And then I was on the carpet, on my knees, bent over that chair, heaving in dry sobs. I couldn't catch my breath.

"I miss my baby," was all I could say, over and over again. I stayed there until there were no tears left—nothing, just the emptiness and the horrible silence of my apartment.

I eventually got up, went into the bathroom, and washed my face with cold water. Then, feeling resolve, I went into the kitchen and started throwing things out. I opened the cupboard and collected an entire shelf of Katie's medicines, shampoos, creams, lotions, you name it, plus the twenty-pound bag of dog food I'd confidently purchased from the vet a few days earlier. I put all this in a plastic garbage bag and took it down to the compactor room. I couldn't look at any of it ever again. Next, I collected Katie's toys, her combs and hairbrushes, the food and water bowls, her coats, her leash, and even the engraved gold Milk-Bone tag that had been around her neck for nearly fifteen years. It read "Katie Plaskin," with her address and phone number etched on it. Every time I heard that little tag rattle on her neck, I knew she was close or in motion, on her way up or down our hall. I decided to keep it on my key chain, so I could always see and hear it, every single day. It's always with me, to this day. I took the rest of Katie's belongings into the large closet in my bedroom and stored it all neatly on the shelves meant for shoes.

After doing all this, I collapsed on the bed and fell into a deep sound sleep.

Later that night, I returned to Pearl's apartment to have a light dinner, but Pearl had no appetite and we sat in the dim light as the sun set, absently listening to the radio. Soon, she returned to bed to watch TV as Naia and I talked quietly in the dining room.

It occurred to me how drastically my relationship with Pearl had changed. For so many years, we were best buddies, surrogate grandmother and grandson, hands-on neighbors, equals—and, above all, Katie's keepers. But now, I had become Pearl's primary caretaker and *de facto* guardian—quite a switch, and not a happy one for me.

Pearl was now dependent rather than independent, as she always had been. This made her vulnerable in a way that turned our world into a melancholy place. I felt her despair. It seemed to hover over her and her apartment.

And yet, I was also deeply touched by her complete trust in me. Just by the way she said my name, or looked at me, or touched me, I knew how much she loved me—that I was truly her son, or her grandson. I wasn't sure which it was—but we were definitely a family. And as in all families, when parents or grandparents get older and frail, it's the children who step in to help.

Granny granted me legal power of attorney, so I now kept track of all her affairs—paid her bills (as her hands shook and she could no longer write a check), paid Naia, and in accordance with her health care proxy, also supervised her medical care. This was more responsibility than I wanted, though being so actively involved made me feel useful, and it also distracted me from Pearl's deteriorating condition.

It was very difficult seeing Oldest increasingly helpless and preparing, in practical ways, for the end. At her request, Lee and I had even gone to the Riverside Funeral Home on Manhattan's Upper West Side to pay for Pearl's funeral in advance. Boy, was that a grim task, picking out a coffin and planning a funeral service for someone who was still alive.

Although I visited Pearl at least two or three times a day to chat and bring her up-to-date on neighborhood news, it was Naia who was Granny's on-the-spot emotional rock, her greatest comfort, tenderly ministering to her every need. We often joked that though Pearl had never come to like Naia's *cooking*, she really loved *Naia*—and treated her like a granddaughter.

Understandably, I could see that Naia was deeply depressed; the weight of caring for a woman in failing health was a heavy burden. Granny noticed it too.

"You're working too hard and losing weight," Granny would fuss, pushing another piece of pie in Naia's direction. "Eat!"

"I love your hair that way, pulled back like a ballerina," she'd tell her. "Why don't you take that brush on the dresser, the one my mother used. It's yours. I don't need it anymore."

"Take a little extra," she said one day, pushing a twenty-dollar bill in Naia's direction, "and treat yourself to a manicure."

"No, Granny," Naia answered firmly, giggling at her ministrations. "I don't need it. But thank you."

At other times, when Pearl's battery ran low, Naia tried her best to rouse her, "Granny, let's take a walk outside." Granny would turn her head away and burrow under the covers just as Katie used to do. "C'mon, sweetheart," Naia urged, "let me help you up." Granny wouldn't budge. We rarely talked about Katie, as it was too painful a subject.

In the weeks and months that followed Katie's death, though, I sensed her presence and lingering spirit around me. I really did. I kept thinking about what Paul had told me before he left—that dogs *want* us to be happy, that they live for it.

Sometimes, especially at night, there was a stir in the air— and I felt her spirit in the room; while at other times, there was nothing but a vast and silent emptiness.

I began to understand that love is not confined to space or time, that it remains and continues on beyond the physical plane. With this comfort, I was able to sleep peacefully most nights; and if I was lucky, Katie would come to visit me in my dreams.

But for Granny, there was little respite from grief. After Katie died, Pearl seemed lost, hibernating under her ancient frayed afghan. No matter what time I walked in to say hello, she was either asleep, depressed and withdrawn, or absently watching TV as if in a trance.

She didn't want to bathe, she ignored the mail, she hardly

ever read, and even had to be persuaded to come to the table for meals. Nothing seemed to cheer her up.

Making matters worse, John announced that he'd gotten a plum five-year assignment at the Paris bureau of his newspaper, so he and Ryan were moving to France. As great an opportunity as it was, Pearl wasn't very happy about the news. It was an effort seeing them since they'd moved uptown, but at least they were still in New York. Now, it would be impossible for her to see them at all.

True, she still had me and Lee and her women friends, but without Katie or Ryan, her heart was broken and she felt more lonesome than ever.

⌐⊃

But in December 2002, a month after Katie's death, I was happy to see Granny at her dining table enjoying a meat loaf dinner complete with fried zucchini and squash, topped off with Chanukah cookies I'd gotten from her favorite Lower East Side bakery, Gertel's.

Her spirits were now somewhat better and she was genuinely pleased and proud when I told her I had just accepted a great job opportunity—ghostwriting a book for someone whom I had long admired.

That was the good news. Unfortunately, this assignment was going to take me away for fifteen months, beginning in March 2003, most of it to be spent in the South Pacific, California, and British Columbia.

"That's wonderful!" exclaimed Granny, hiding her true feelings as she handed me a frosted dreidel cookie. "But what are we going to do without you here?"

The plan was for Naia to continue taking care of Pearl while the indispensable Lee would visit her as much as possible. I'd call her most every day. Even so, I knew it was going to be difficult for Pearl. Still, I admit I was excited to be leaving New York for an extended period, relieved to get away from our now-depressing hallway and the Battery Park City winters to see another part of the world, especially the South Pacific.

Yet, as I packed my new laptop and four suitcases for the overseas trip, I felt guilty about leaving Pearl, though I completely trusted Naia to cope without me.

On the big departure day, I came into Pearl's bedroom to say good-bye and gave her a big hug. "Now Granny, you be *good*!—and don't drive poor Naia crazy."

"I will so!" she answered mischievously, holding my arm tightly. And then, stoic as ever, she waved good-bye as I blew her a kiss.

"Have a great time—and *call* me!" And I was off on my great adventure.

⤜⤏

Although I came home periodically between trips, I was immersed in work and often distracted, while Pearl seemed more withdrawn than ever. I was fully aware that my absence had shrunk her world (and her support system) more and more. I was especially grateful that Lee was taking Pearl out to lunch, out for walks, and was even kind enough to get my mail and pay my bills (and Granny's) while I was away.

"When I first met Pearl," Lee reflected, "I could tell that she was not a person who had been embraced very much. There had not been much physical warmth in her life. I began hugging and kissing her and stroking her hand. At first, she'd be very stiff. But especially after Katie died, she started hugging back.

"Every time I'd leave her bedroom, I'd always say, 'I love you, Pearlie Girlie,' and she'd just look at me. But one time when I was leaving and forgot to hug and kiss her good-bye, she said, 'Oh, what? No kiss?!' It wasn't long after that that she started telling me, 'I love you' back."

That spring, I had a great birthday party at home, inviting the new friends I'd met in Australia and Palm Springs. Granny uncharacteristically never made her usual cameo appearance for dessert. She just wasn't in the mood, her party girl days seemingly over.

And in the late fall of 2003, although Oldest could still walk indoors as long as Naia supported her, she started using a wheelchair for trips outside the apartment as her balance was unsteady.

One day, when I was home from a trip, I ran into them both outside by the bank, which was the first time I had seen Pearl out and about in the chair. I sensed that being in it publicly embarrassed her, violating her pride.

From my vantage point, seeing her disabled this way was heartbreaking. Granny looked frail and vulnerable. But there was also something brave about her that day. Her hair was brushed back as it blew in the blustery Battery wind. Her face was made-up (thanks to Naia), and she was nicely dressed with a jaunty orange silk scarf at her neck. Touchingly, although she seemed dazed and more passive than usual, she was still pleased to run into neighbors she knew, asking questions and smiling, making comments and witty remarks.

She was still Granny, just slowed down—and deeply sad.

She had lost so much in sixteen years—her husband, John and Ryan, Katie, and now, in a sense, me as well, as I was so often out of town.

During this period, she even confided to John that she sometimes prayed to die. "She didn't understand why God was keeping her alive—and wanted to be with Arthur," he recalled.

"What's the point of being here?" she had once asked me in despair.

"Granny!" I exclaimed, trying to make light of that heart-rending question, though I fully understood it. "You have us, you know you do."

She just looked at me that day, changing the subject. Most of the time, she kept the banter light between us, protectively hiding her despair from me.

Sure, we spoke all the time and saw each other, but it just wasn't the same. When I'd call Pearl from the Gold Coast of Australia or from Palm Springs, she sounded distant and lost, and sometimes confused. Her voice was no longer booming and filled with curiosity. It was flat, softer, and distracted.

"Pearl had a broken heart," said her friend Rose. "Everything was getting to be too much for her. She said her biggest disappointment was feeling that she was no longer needed."

I wondered if Granny was mad at me. "Mad no, sad yes," Rose later told me. "She was just lonely. You were the child she never had. She told me that."

When I heard this, I knew it was time to head home.

CHAPTER TWENTY-FIVE

Love Remains

In June 2004, I was finally finished with the book I'd been ghostwriting and flew in from Palm Springs, relieved to be back again in Battery Park City rather than baking in the 110-degree temperatures of the desert.

The summer weather here was spectacular. The Hudson River, as usual, was brimming with sailboats catching the breeze, and the Esplanade was filled with bikers, joggers, and dozens of happy dogs.

All of it was a comforting welcome home and I was looking forward to a relaxing holiday—and to being with Pearl.

"Hello Granny!" I exclaimed, bursting into her bedroom and giving her a big hug and some presents—including a little bamboo clock I'd found in California along with some chocolate-covered coconuts.

"My boy is home!" she smiled wanly, struggling to sit up in bed.

"You remember me, Oldest?"

"Barely," she answered.

"No, no, she can't have those, her stomach isn't so good," Naia told me under her breath as she took the candies away.

"So, tell me all about your trip—and if you've got any other presents there for me," Granny laughed.

After we talked for a while, I made an excuse to go out into the living room.

"She's sick again," whispered Naia, who looked ready to burst with stress, having been alone with Granny day after day with little time for rest.

"It's the diverticulitis," she explained, the same disease that had landed Pearl in the hospital in 2001.

"What are the symptoms?" I asked her.

"Same as last time—the belly pain, bloating, constipation, and chills."

Even with Naia's vigilant care, I could see that Pearl was far worse than the last time I'd seen her. She looked ghostly white, she'd lost more weight, and her hands were cold even with the *heat* turned on high in June, making the room suffocating.

As Naia and I talked, she told me that the trend had continued, with Pearl rarely getting out of bed and sleeping the days away. She often had bad dreams or hallucinations caused by the brain tumor.

More and more, Pearl escaped into her own little world, talking to Arthur out loud as she drifted in and out of long naps. It had been ten years now since he died, "but she was dreaming about him all the time," her friend Rose remembered. "She knew time was running out and told me that it was almost like Arthur was calling to her, waiting for her. She was looking forward to seeing him on the other side."

Naia, sensitive to Pearl's loneliness, tried her best to keep her spirits up, but it just wasn't working. Neither was the medicine.

More than anything, it was Pearl's stomach that was the ongoing problem.

"I give her prunes and raisins and cook special foods for

her, pureeing them and feeding her by hand," said Naia, "but nothing seems to help."

Although Pearl's primary care physician was trying various approaches to alleviate Pearl's problem, she wasn't improving. And by the fall of 2004, Pearl was bleeding internally. Although she was scheduled to have a colonoscopy, she wasn't up to doing the preparation necessary for the procedure.

Then one afternoon in early October, just a week after her ninety-second birthday, Naia called me in a panic. "Please! It's Granny. Come over. Now!"

As I entered the bedroom, Pearl was in bed lying on her back, but very still. Naia was close to tears and talking rapidly. "This morning she was very weak and couldn't talk much. Now she's passed out. She's breathing, but like in a coma. And her pressure is very low."

We called 911 and within minutes, a fireman and two ER technicians were in Pearl's bedroom, putting an IV in her arm and an oxygen mask over her face. With Pearl on a stretcher, we took a somber elevator ride to the lobby, then into the ambulance and off to St. Vincent's Hospital. As the siren blared away, I sat in the back holding Granny's hand, talking to her about—who else?—Katie.

"Granny, remember when Katie used to steal the cake right after you baked it?" She opened her eyes and gave me a little nod of her head. "Naughty girl," she whispered.

Late in the day, after Pearl was settled in her hospital room, her physician called me out into the hall. He knew that I had the medical power of attorney and a health care proxy that had a "do not resuscitate" order in it, as Pearl wanted no extraordinary measures taken to prolong her life, a subject we had discussed in the past.

"The MRI shows that Pearl has a total obstruction of the

bowel" he told me. "She'll require immediate surgery to correct it—within the next twenty-four hours."

"And if she doesn't have it?" I asked.

He paused. "If she doesn't do it, her condition is fatal. So you need to discuss this with her now."

"I would rather have you explain it to her."

"I think you should do it," he said.

"But you're the doctor," I insisted.

In the end, as the doctor refused to speak to Pearl, I walked back into Granny's room and lightly touched her arm, trying to wake her up. I dreaded this moment. She was very groggy, only half-conscious, though I could tell she was able to hear and understand me.

"Granny!" I said fairly loudly. "I need to talk to you. I just spoke to your doctor, and he told me that you need an operation on your stomach...can you hear me?"

And she shook her head yes.

"The doctor says that—you need it now...that if you don't do it..." I paused because I didn't want to say the next words.

"If you don't do it, Granny, he said you could die. Do you understand?"

She shook her head yes again.

"So...Granny, do you want the operation?"

Given the choice between extending her life or death, what would she do? I knew the answer.

Ever so slowly, Pearl opened up her eyes and shook her head no.

"Are you sure you don't want it, because you can get it."

She shook her head again.

"Okay," I said, gently holding her hand. And she had a surprisingly strong grip on it. "Then, don't worry. We won't do it. Just rest."

I understood that Pearl couldn't bear having her body disturbed by one more doctor. It reminded me of the suffering Katie had endured and how she was ready to slip away when she could.

I sat by Pearl's bed in a daze. My mind drifted away, back in time, rewinding our adventures of the last sixteen years. All of it came flooding back from the first day I knocked on Pearl's door.

There was my bowlegged puppy arriving in Battery Park City, climbing in Pearl's lap and falling soundly asleep. Then she was outside by the Hudson River, curiously looking out at the ships as Pearl fed her a pistachio ice-cream cone. I saw Katie's paw resting possessively on Pa-Re-El's arm as Granny whispered confidentially into her ear. "Girlie, you look so pretty!"

The bond between them had been unshakeable. And even two years after Katie's passing, Pearl never stopped talking or thinking about her girl. Their love was eternal.

I saw Pearl handing me her plum tart baked especially for Katharine Hepburn, a look of pride and excitement on her face as she wrapped it in Saran Wrap for the trip uptown. There she was sitting at the table in her Donald Duck hat, giggling with Ryan as they played Fish; wiping Ryan's chocolate-covered mouth with a napkin; picking him up at the bus; putting on a Halloween mask as she went trick-or-treating with him; and tenderly tucking him into bed.

I saw Oldest laughing when she tasted that disastrous cake I'd made, pointing out that I'd accidentally put in salt instead of sugar; hurrying into the hospital ward after my bike accident; bringing hot chicken soup into my bedroom the following day; energetically walking Katie when I couldn't; toweling Katie dry after a walk in the rain; and holding onto my arm firmly as we made our way through the mud to Arthur's funeral.

And I could never forget Katie, Pearl, John, and Ryan posing together for *Family Circle* and Pearl later sitting at her dining table reading the "Granny Down the Hall" article, distributing it to all her friends. I felt her hand firmly on my shoulder, so proud.

In this kaleidoscope of happy memories, I saw Pearl's cameo appearances at parties, making her entrance (as Katie poked behind her legs) as I announced, "Heeeeeeeeeeeeere's Granny!"

I heard her advice, her opinions, and most of all, her laughter.

"Thirsty," she told me now, her lips parched.

"She can't drink any water," the nurse told me, "but I'll bring you some ice chips that you can give her."

She handed me shaved ice on little wooden sticks. I went over to Pearl's bedside and held one of them in her mouth as she sucked away on it, grateful to keep her lips moist. She seemed a little more alert.

"Let's call Lee and you can say hello," I told her. Granny nodded her head.

I put the call through on my cell phone and held it up to her ear, "Pearlie, are you okay? Are you in pain?" Lee asked.

"No, I'm okay," Pearl whispered, almost inaudible. "How are you?"

"I'm fine. Pearlie, are you having a hard time talking?"

"Yes."

"Then just listen. Glenn will be back in the morning, and I'll see you in the afternoon." Lee began to cry, silently, sensing that this could be their last call.

"I love you, Pearlie Girlie."

"I love you too."

"I'll see you later," she said.

A few minutes later, I said good night to Granny and headed home from the hospital. "Okay, Granny," I said, holding her hand. "I'm going to go now and I'll see you tomorrow morning."

She looked up at me and nodded.

And that was the last time I ever saw Pearl.

⌬

That morning, October 18, 2004, at about 3:00 a.m., I was startled when my phone rang. I picked up the receiver, half asleep. It was a male nurse from St. Vincent's whom I had met earlier that day. "I'm sorry to tell you that your friend Pearl passed away a few minutes ago."

"How?" I asked.

"She had no pain. She just fell asleep, stopped breathing."

So this was it. Death is strange. One minute, the person you love is right there, holding your hand, sick but breathing and alive. Then they're gone.

In a way, I was relieved. Granny was free. All the suffering was over.

She'd been lost in profound sadness since Katie's death, sleeping the days away or endlessly watching TV, waiting for the end to come. A horrible silence had enveloped her household for months at a time, what with John and Ryan long gone and me so often away.

And now, at the ripe age of ninety-two, Granny could rest in peace.

I went into my dining room, where I kept all the leather-bound scrapbooks, twenty of them lined up along a built-in bookcase, each organized by theme ("Granny's Eighty-fifth Party," "Katie the Wonder Dog," "Halloween," "Valentine's

Day," etc.). I pulled out the biggest book, a red one, filled with pictures of Granny, Katie, Ryan, John, and me.

I took it into bed with me, and spent the rest of the night turning page after page as the story of our lives came back to life in complete detail. In two of the most poignant pictures, I saw Pearl holding Ryan's hand, and years later, Naia holding *Pearl's* hand, each supporting and protecting the other.

How fortunate we all were to have found in Pearl a mother, grandmother, friend, confidante, and neighbor—all rolled into one. And how blessed we were to have been brought together by Katie.

At daybreak, the first person I called with the news of Granny's passing was Lee, who had returned to town from New Jersey with the intention of seeing Pearl at the hospital. After a very brief phone conversation, Lee came up to my apartment. When I opened the door, she stood there, crushed and incredibly sad. For just a moment, we looked at each other, and then she fell into my arms, crying, bereft that her Pearlie Girlie was gone.

After a few minutes together, we went down to Granny's apartment to break the news to Naia. She was inconsolable. She had spent over two years, day and night, taking care of Granny, and they had become incredibly close.

"I felt terrible," Naia later told me. "Pearl and I were so attached...it was overwhelming to lose her."

As Naia had no home of her own, I asked if she'd like to stay on for a while in Pearl's apartment. But she shook her head no, bent over at the dining table sobbing as Lee held her in her arms. I looked around the apartment, at Granny's wheelchair, at the medicine bottles, and at the empty twin bed that she'd left just the day before. I looked at all the little knickknacks

Pearl loved, her prized collection of Broadway programs and cookbooks, and her healthy plants lovingly tended to along the windowsill. It all seemed desolate without her there.

The next day, when Lee and I got to the funeral home, we entered the chapel to say our final good-byes. Although I dreaded seeing Granny, she looked very much at peace, lovely really. Her face was beautiful.

Into her coffin, Lee placed the cherished honeymoon photo of a very young Pearl and Arthur out for a stroll on the boardwalk in Atlantic City. She also put in Pearl's porcelain doll and the afghan her mother had knitted, both of which had given her such comfort. And finally, I stepped forward to put in a framed picture of Katie, the one taken at Granny's eighty-fifth birthday party, where she sat happily in Pearl's arms, outfitted in one of her party dresses. Now they could rest together.

At the Westchester cemetery, there were about twenty-five people, a mix of Pearl's relatives, friends, and neighbors, including Lee, Naia, Paul, and Rose, plus my sister Debby, who loved Pearl and came in from Albany for it. I was especially glad that John and Ryan were coincidentally in the United States on a short visit and able to be there. What a bittersweet reunion. Ryan was somber and, at age thirteen, looked so handsome and grown up. I think this was probably his first brush with death, and he was very brave about it. I know how much he loved Granny.

John spoke poignantly of Pearl, about her strength and pragmatic spirit, her warmth and giving nature, and how she gave John and Ryan a second home when they most needed one. "She always made time for us, even when Arthur was sick—and after he died, she adopted us both.

"Pa-Re-El became my confidante and never hesitated to express her point of view when she thought I was messing up!"

he added with a laugh. He reminded us of her steady calmness, her constant willingness to help, and her funny and fun-loving nature. "We will miss her terribly," he finished.

Lee then spoke of Pearl, whom she described as "a woman of today—strong, independent, with a wit as sharp as a tack. And she used it until the last days of her life, keeping us in line when we needed it."

"Pearl," she added, "was quick to point out our shortcomings, but always in a humorous and loving way. It was on September 11 that I found Pearl, alone and confused. There was an immediate bond forged amid the horror of the day, which grew and sustained our friendship. I was always hugging and kissing her and I know she loved it. We will miss you, Pearlie Girlie."

Then Rose, who had so faithfully supported Pearl in her final days, stepped forward with a poignant poem about God calling Pearl home, "though she will never be alone," said Rose, "because part of us went with her."

As I stood there on that crisp sunny October morning, I felt content to let other people have their say about Granny. I had nothing I really wanted to say myself, not that day, and not in public.

As all families do, we were now experiencing the inevitable loss that comes with illness and death. But I was somehow numb to the sadness that day as I found myself gazing up at the trees and rolling hills of the cemetery.

Knowing Pearl's love of nature, I was thinking she would have taken special pleasure in the beautiful Japanese maples, oaks, and dogwoods now surrounding her.

It would take time for me to fully understand the grand pattern of what had happened over sixteen years and what it all meant. All I knew was that I missed Oldest, my closest friend and Katie's keeper, and that she would never be far from my mind, just as Katie never was.

As I looked up at the sky, I imagined my dog's spirit somewhere up there merging with her beloved Granny, both together at last, with Katie snuggled up against Pearl, the two of them blissfully content.

An Open Door

During the next few months, I was leveled by the loss. It felt like the final blow, with Granny, Katie, and Arthur gone, while John and Ryan were back again in Paris, our reunion all too brief. Even Naia, whom I was so fond of, was leaving. Everyone had moved on...but I was still here living along the hallway that was now eerily quiet.

Although Ryan and John would periodically keep in touch, the unique closeness we once felt could never be captured again. Partly because of the geographical distance that separated us, there was no chance of holding onto what we'd had. And the matriarch of our family and Katie were both gone—twin spirits that had kept us all united.

After just a few months, though, I concentrated less on what I had lost, less on the past, and more on *appreciating* the gift that had been given to me.

I saw that what I had experienced was the abiding love of family—in the form that I had found it—a singularly happy living situation that could not last forever—but one that lives always within its surviving members.

So although our family, in a physical sense, could not

survive the inevitability of death and changing circumstances, the memory of our unique bond could never be forgotten.

The lesson in all this, for me, was a simple one: *LOVE REMAINS*.

It always does. It always will.

It lives on firmly in my heart and in John's and in Ryan's— and in Lee, Rose, Paul, and Naia—and in Katie's beloved Ramon and her lifetime groomer Betty.

I hear each of their voices so clearly, and see, in flashback, the entire movie of our lives together.

Nowadays, each morning at 10:00 a.m., a lanky young man with brown curly hair can be found walking along the Right Bank of the Seine with his two dogs, Jacqui, an assertive black teacup poodle ("the boss") and Chance, a mellow white-and-brown-spotted papillon.

He's laughing as the spunky dogs pull him along, steering him toward a neighborhood patisserie, where he buys a chocolate croissant.

"No, chocolate isn't good for dogs," he lectures the hungry canines, instead feeding them a cinnamon palmier, a puff pastry with granulated sugar. This young man with the deep baritone voice is *Ryan*! And I can barely juxtapose the boisterous, plump-cheeked boy I remember so well with this mature, rather poised nineteen-year-old.

Thankfully, John reports back all about Ryan in our biweekly phone conversations, catch-ups that have gone on ever since John and Ryan moved to Paris six years ago.

It wasn't so long ago that "the kid," as I still think of him, was walking Katie along the Hudson River in Battery Park City.

Oh, how I miss Ryan barreling into my apartment, unhitching Katie's leash and wildly chasing after my dog, whipping up bubbles in the tub, or getting chocolate all over his face.

But time moves on. John works as an editor for the *International Herald Tribune* and is entirely content in Paris with a new partner, not likely to come back to the United States anytime soon. I really wish he would.

Ryan, a master of computer games, graduated from the International School of Paris and has plans to continue his studies in Japan and California. While I remember him as a bubbly, talkative kid who challenged Katie to hallway races and soccer matches, he's now thoughtful and introspective, rather shy and sweetly sensitive.

"I always thought of Pearl as my grandmother, of course," he recently told me via Skype, peering into the camera lens and waving.

"We talked about a lot of stuff. She read to me, played cards with me, picked me up from school at the bus...liked spoiling me with her chocolate pie, and brought home all those baked goods. Then Katie would stick her nose into the boxes trying to steal the goodies. She kissed me a lot, always licking my face, and I remember how she cheated in races!"—all of it a bittersweet gift that none of us will ever forget.

As for me, I should tell you that I still live in the same apartment on the third floor overlooking the Hudson River. So I pass by Granny's door all the time. Sometimes it's kind of spooky. It feels like the ghost of what had been still lingers there. There's even the mezuzah, a Hebrew prayer scroll, still attached outside her door—the one put there by Arthur twenty-seven years ago, a reminder of his strong faith.

But I'm quickly brought back to the present by the rap music blasting from her apartment. Ironically, a young disc jockey has moved in. (What would Granny think of *that*!?) Seeing him go in and out of "her" apartment is a little surreal. Sometimes, when I can, I steal a glimpse inside when he opens his front door, curiously wanting to recapture, for just a moment, what had taken place within those rooms.

But it doesn't really matter whether or not I go inside that apartment ever again, for what happened there is inside *me*.

Indeed, the story that began in a little town built on water would never be forgotten. It was probably a once-in-a-lifetime happening, and nothing like it will ever unfold in quite the same way again.

I've come to believe that the events that unfolded here were not just random or coincidental, but rather somehow guided by a higher, providential force. I don't pretend to understand it—but I do feel it all around me.

I often think of that phrase about *opportunity knocking*—and see it at work every day. Things seem to happen when the timing is right, and I have faith that this will always be true.

I sometimes ask myself, how did I find the right dog breeder who just happened to have an unwanted puppy? Why did I "accidentally" meet Pearl, or come upon John and Ryan by a chance encounter on that cold January day at the Community Center?

In my heart, I now know that this string of seemingly unrelated events were gifts, *invitations* from a higher power that led me to taking a step forward—to taking a chance.

And I believe that Granny and Arthur, John and Ryan, and my Katie were just such gifts.

Nowadays, without them, our hallway is, of course, a lot lonelier and the vacuum left behind has not always been easy to cope with. Yet it's funny how new friendships develop and old ones deepen when we most need them to.

Instead of Granny, I'm now incredibly close to my neighbor Linda, on the eighteenth floor, who had always been in the background of my life until we got involved in our neighborhood tenants' association. She's a rock—witty, irreverent, and supportive—a daily source of wise counsel and laughter.

Then there's my unofficial "life coach" and confidante Peg on the eighth floor, who is, coincidentally, my sister's best friend. With her soothing voice and buoyant spirit, "Peggsy" has that rare ability to put everything into perspective no matter what the day has thrown at me.

Twenty floors up from Peg is my screenwriting partner Brandon, his young wife Sheila, their two toddlers, Merrick and Rhys, and a perky Maltese named Fred. Their home has become yet another warm harbor, filled with lively conversation and baby mayhem.

And literally across the hall from me is my ninety-four-year-old neighbor Freda ("your local sage!" she laughs), the retired judge mentioned earlier who had polio as a child. (Katie always sensitively avoided jumping up on her legs.) Freda and I were always cordial but never especially close; but with Granny gone, we've developed a deep connection—trading stories (and dark chocolate bars), celebrating precious birthdays, and looking out for one another.

And on it goes.

No matter what blessings may or may not come my way in the future, I realize that I have already had *plenty*. God has been good to me.

After all, some people never experience the good fortune that I did. And every time I look at one of my scrapbooks, or walk outside on the Esplanade, or sit on Pearl's favorite park bench, or see another cocker spaniel trotting by—the entire story I've told you comes flooding back to me.

I often tell my friends that maybe, right at this moment, there's somebody down *their* hallway or across the street just waiting to open their door to you. I never did understand the idea of neighbors staying apart from one another.

And neither did the incomparable Katie, who always broke down any door she could paw her way into!

In fact, she owned our hallway, and her greatest pleasure was running up and down it, herding us all together.

That was her gift, a legacy I gratefully pass on, from one dog lover to another, indeed to everyone.

Create Your Own Tail of Love

Glenn's Favorite Dog and Animal Charities

AMERICAN KENNEL CLUB

The nation's only not-for-profit registry promotes responsible dog ownership, donates millions to canine health research, assists with disaster relief, and provides purebred rescue grants through its AKC Humane Fund; www.akc.org

ANIMAL MEDICAL CENTER

A nonprofit veterinary hospital that promotes the health of companion animals through advanced treatment, research, and education; provides free veterinary care to guide dogs and subsidized health care for the pets of the indigent elderly; www.amcny.org

ASPCA

The first U.S. humane organization established to fight against cruelty to animals, rescue animals from abuse, and share resources with shelters nationwide; www.ASPCA.org

BROADWAY BARKS

Created by Bernadette Peters and Mary Tyler Moore; fosters the adoption of homeless animals; promotes community spirit among shelter and rescue groups; www.broadwaybarks.com

CESAR AND ILUSION MILLAN FOUNDATION

Delivers humane education programs and promotes animal welfare by supporting the rescue, rehabilitation, and re-homing of abused and abandoned dogs; www.millanfoundation.org

GUIDE DOGS FOR THE BLIND

Provides guide dogs throughout the United States and Canada for the blind and visually impaired at no cost; www.guidedogs.com

HUMANE SOCIETY OF NEW YORK

A no-kill shelter that rescues abandoned animals and places them for adoption; offers low-cost hospital services; www .humanesocietyny.org

HUMANE SOCIETY OF THE UNITED STATES

Seeks a humane world for all animals and fights against cruelty, exploitation, and neglect, advocating new public policies and working to enforce existing laws; www.humanesociety.org

MORRIS ANIMAL FOUNDATION

Improves the health and longevity of companion animals and wildlife by funding humane health studies to advance veterinary medicine; www.morrisanimalfoundation.org

NORTH SHORE ANIMAL LEAGUE AMERICA

The world's largest no-kill shelter dedicated to rescuing, nurturing, and adopting as many dogs, cats, puppies, and kittens as possible; www.nsalamerica.org

PEDIGREE FOUNDATION

Dedicated to helping the four million dogs in U.S. shelters find loving homes by providing grants to 501(c)(3) animal shelters and rescue groups; www.pedigreefoundation.org

ABOUT THE AUTHOR

Veteran journalist and celebrity interviewer **GLENN PLASKIN** is the bestselling author of *Horowitz: The Biography of Vladimir Horowitz* and *Turning Point: Pivotal Moments in the Lives of America's Celebrities*. His profiles and columns have appeared in the *New York Times*, the *Daily News*, *San Francisco Chronicle*, *Los Angeles Times*, *Chicago Tribune*, *Family Circle*, *US Weekly*, *Ladies Home Journal*, *Cosmopolitan*, *W*, and *Playboy*. His interview subjects have included such figures as Katharine Hepburn, Nancy Reagan, Calvin Klein, Senator Edward Kennedy, Audrey Hepburn, Elizabeth Taylor, Leona Helmsley, Barbara Walters, Diane Sawyer, Donald Trump, Al Pacino, and Meryl Streep. His TV appearances include *The Today Show*, *Oprah*, and *Larry King Live*. He lives in New York City. Visit the author's websites at www.glennplaskin.com and www.katiebook.com.

AMERICAN
KENNEL CLUB®

Advocating for the purebred dog as a family companion, advancing canine health and well-being, working to protect the rights of all dog owners and promoting responsible dog ownership, the **American Kennel Club:**

Sponsors more than **22,000 sanctioned events** annually including conformation, agility, obedience, rally, tracking, lure coursing, earthdog, herding, field trial, hunt test, and coonhound events

Features a **10-step Canine Good Citizen® program** that rewards dogs who have good manners at home and in the community

Has reunited more than **370,000** lost pets with their owners through the AKC Companion Animal Recovery - visit **www.akccar.org**

Created and supports the AKC Canine Health Foundation, which funds research projects using the more than **$22 million** the AKC has donated since 1995 - visit **www.caninehealthfoundation.org**

Joins **animal lovers** through education, outreach and grant-making via the AKC Humane Fund - visit **www.akchumanefund.org**

We're more than champion dogs. We're the dog's champion.

www.akc.org